English Skills 1

Answers

Carol Matchett

Schofield & Sims

Which book?

The **English Skills** books are aligned with the end-of-year objectives for Key Stage 2. For the majority of pupils aged seven to 11 years, follow the guidance given on page 2 as to which book to use with each year group.

If a pupil is working significantly above or below the standard normally expected for his or her age, another book may be more appropriate. If you are not sure which to choose, **Workbook descriptors** and a simple **Entry test** are available to help you identify the book that is best suited to the pupil's abilities. You can also use these resources with new pupils joining your class or school.

Photocopy masters of the **Workbook descriptors** and **Entry test** are provided in the **Teacher's Guide** – which also contains the **Entry test marking key**, full instructions for use, and a range of other **English Skills** copymasters. For ordering details, see page 46.

You may be using **English Skills** at Key Stage 3 or with other mixed-ability groups of young people or adults. In such cases you will find the **Workbook descriptors** and **Entry test** vital in deciding which book to give each student.

Published by Schofield & Sims Ltd,
Dogley Mill, Fenay Bridge, Huddersfield HD8 0NQ, UK
Telephone 01484 607080

www.schofieldandsims.co.uk

Copyright © Schofield and Sims Ltd, 2011

Author: Carol Matchett
Carol Matchett has asserted her moral right under the Copyright, Designs and Patents Act, 1988, to be identified as the author of this work.

British Library Cataloguing in Publication Data
A catalogue record for this book is available from the British Library.

Commissioning and editorial project management by
Carolyn Richardson Publishing Services *(www.publiserve.co.uk)*

*Design by **Ledgard Jepson Ltd***
*Printed in the UK by **Wyndeham Gait Ltd**, Grimsby, Lincolnshire*

Book 1 Answers ISBN 978 07217 1181 2

Contents

Schofield & Sims English Skills 1 Answers

Teacher's notes

Introduction to the series

Schofield & Sims English Skills provides regular and carefully graded practice in key literacy skills. It is designed for use alongside your existing literacy lessons, embedding key aspects of grammar, sentence structure, punctuation and spelling and constantly revisiting them until they become automatic. At the same time it reinforces and develops pupils' knowledge of word structure and vocabulary.

Each workbook comprises three sections with 12 tests in each one. The tests become more difficult, but the increase in difficulty is gradual. The workbooks are fully compatible with the Key Stage 2 literacy curriculum and the final tests in each book are aligned with the end-of-year objectives as follows:

- **Book 1:** Year 2
- **Book 2:** Year 3
- **Book 3:** Year 4
- **Book 4:** Year 5
- **Book 5:** Year 6
- **Book 6:** Years 6/7

Please note: Pupils working towards the objectives for an earlier year should use the appropriate workbook. There is no need for all members of the class to be working on the same book at the same time.

Parts A, B and C

Each test is divided into three parts:

- Part A: **Warm-up** – puzzles, 'warm-up' exercises and revision of earlier learning
- Part B: **Word work** – spelling, word structure, exploring words and their meanings
- Part C: **Sentence work** – putting words together to make sentences: for example, choosing suitable words, forming and punctuating sentences or checking for grammatical accuracy.

Answering the test questions

After you have demonstrated to the class how some of the different question types are to be answered, the pupils work through the test items without adult help – either individually or in pairs. For Books 2 to 6, encourage them to refer to dictionaries, thesauruses and other reference materials rather than asking for your help. The tests may be used flexibly. For example, a test may be tackled in one session or over several days.

Marking

This book provides correct answers for **English Skills 1**; where various different answers would be acceptable, an example is provided. The **Focus** panel stating the areas of learning being tested helps you to decide whether the pupil's answer is satisfactory. **Please note and explain to the class that if all or part of a question has several possible answers, the question number is displayed like this** 5 . **If a question has a specific answer, the question number is displayed like this** 5 . **It is displayed in this way even if the answer is made up of several parts that may be given in any order.**

Some questions test more than one area: for example, a question on writing in the past tense might also check pupils' knowledge of the spelling rules for adding **ed**. In such cases, both parts of the answer must be correct, reflecting real-life situations that require varied knowledge and skills.

Group marking sessions

Group or class marking sessions led by the teacher or classroom assistant are the most effective way of marking the tests: pupils learn by comparing and discussing answers.

Another benefit of group or class marking sessions is that they highlight deficits in pupils' knowledge, which will inform your future teaching. Where pupils have given a wrong answer, or none at all, briefly reinforce the key teaching point using an item from this book as a model. In a plenary discussion at the end of the session, encourage pupils to evaluate their own successes; each pupil can then work with a 'talk partner' to record areas needing improvement and discuss appropriate learning objectives.

Marking the end-of-section assessments

At the end of each workbook section are two writing assessments: the independent writing task and the proofreading task. These check that pupils are applying in their writing the knowledge, skills and understanding developed in the weekly tests. The assessments also provide evidence of a pupil's strengths and weaknesses, which will help you to set appropriate targets. You might consider sharing with the pupils a simplified version of the mark scheme – and then involve them in setting their own targets, as discussed above.

- ### The independent writing task

The independent writing task gives you a snapshot of a pupil's writing development. Prompts help pupils to plan and gather ideas so that when they begin writing they can focus on expressing their ideas clearly and effectively. On pages 16, 30 and 44 you will find photocopiable **Writing task assessment sheets** – one for each section – with specific assessment points arranged under the headings 'Sentence structure and punctuation', 'Composition and effect' and 'Spelling'. Complete one of these sheets as you mark each pupil's work.

- ### The proofreading task

The proofreading task focuses on punctuation, grammar and spelling. Examples of **Completed proofreading tasks** for each section, also photocopiable, are supplied on pages 17, 31 and 45. However, please note that pupils may choose to correct some of the errors using methods different to those shown in the example but equally valid. For example, two unpunctuated strings of words might be joined using a connective or separated to make two sentences. Additional evidence gained from the relevant proofreading task will help you to further assess pupils' achievements in 'Sentence punctuation' and 'Spelling' as already assessed in the writing task. If you wish, you can use the photocopiable sheet to make notes on a pupil's work.

Please note: Pupils whose scores against the assessment statements are low do not need to repeat a section. All the books revisit difficult areas and offer ample opportunities for further practice. Instead of holding a pupil back, highlight the assessment statements that reveal his or her weaknesses and use these to set learning targets. Ensure that pupils know their targets as they begin the next section.

Progress chart

On page 46 of the pupil workbook only you will find a **Progress chart**, with one column each for Sections 1, 2 and 3, and a list of 'I can' statements relating to the kinds of activities practised in the section. Please ask every pupil to complete the relevant column when they have finished working through a section.

The **Progress chart** encourages pupils to monitor their own work by identifying those activities that they have mastered and those requiring further attention. When pupils colour in the chart as recommended (**green** for **easy**, **orange** for **getting there** and **red** for **difficult**) it gives a clear picture of progress. It also shows the benefits of systematic practice: an activity that the pupil cannot perform in Section 1 later gets the 'green light'.

The **Progress chart** promotes assessment for learning and personalised learning. Whilst it is best completed in the workbook, so that achievements in all sections may be compared, you may at some point wish to have additional copies. For this reason, it may be photocopied. **However, all other pages of the pupil workbook remain strictly non-photocopiable.**

Section 1   Test 1

A   WARM-UP

Write a word that rhymes with **day**.

1 bay

2 hay

3 pay

4 play

> **PART A Focus**
> **1–4:** rhyme; phonemes (check for irregular spellings)
> **5:** sentence structure
> **6–8:** segmenting phonemes
> **9–10:** sentence structure; sentence punctuation

5 Make the words into a sentence.

boy The went home.

The boy went home.

Add the missing letters.

6 b u n c h of flowers

7 s t a m p your feet

8 s t a n d up

9 Write a sentence using the word **frog**.

The frog jumped into the pool.

10 Write a sentence using the word **pet**.

I have a pet dog.

B   WORD WORK

Add the missing letters.

ee ea

1 s p e a k

2 d r e a m

3 s t r e e t

> **PART B Focus**
> **1–6:** alternative spellings of **long e** phoneme
> **7–8:** high-frequency words; visual spelling skills
> **9–10:** language choice; description

Use the words in these sentences.

4 This is the street where I live.

5 I can't hear you. Speak up.

6 Last night I had a dream .

Underline the correct spelling.

7 sor saw sorr suw

8 yur your yoor yor

Write three words to describe

9 **a banana**

yellow curved soft

10 **an apple**

crisp red shiny

C   SENTENCE WORK

Finish the sentence.

1 Nikki went to visit her friend.

2 The big dog barked at the cat.

3 The ball went over the fence.

4 Mr Smith is going shopping.

Change one word so that the sentence makes sense. Write the new word. Cross out the old one.

5 Come back ~~an~~ help me. and

6 Simon ~~wet~~ to see the old lady. went

7 In the garden we ~~was~~ two magpies. saw

> **PART C Focus**
> **1–4:** sentence structure; full stops
> **5–7:** rereading for accuracy and common errors
> **8–10:** capital letters

Write the sentence again but with capital letters in the correct places.

8 gemma and jack came to my party. Gemma and Jack came to my party.

9 my teacher is called mr henderson. My teacher is called Mr Henderson.

10 today i am going to jordan's house. Today I am going to Jordan's house.

X DEFINITIVE ANSWER   X SAMPLE ANSWER

Section 1 Test 2

A WARM-UP

The beginnings and endings of these sentences are mixed up.

The boy   opened.
The door   hissed.
The snake   grinned.

Write the sentences correctly.

1 _The boy grinned._
2 _The door opened._
3 _The snake hissed._

Write three words that rhyme with the word in **bold**.

4 **dust**   _just_   _rust_   _crust_
5 **jump**   _bump_   _lump_   _thump_
6 **damp**   _camp_   _lamp_   _stamp_

Add a letter to make a new word.

7 s e e _d_
8 t o o _k_
9 b e e _f_
10 t e a _m_

PART A Focus
1–3: sentences must make sense
4–6: rhyme; CVCC words
7–10: phonemes

B WORD WORK

Add the missing letters to make words that rhyme with **late**.

a i e

1 s k _a_ t _e_   3 w _a_ i t
2 p l _a_ t _e_   4 _e_ _i_ g h t

5 Add a letter to make three new words.

the _m_   the _n_   the _y_

Use the new words in these sentences.

6 Help _them_ to carry it.
7 _They_ are late.
8 Just _then_ it stopped raining.

Write three things you might see at the seaside and three things you might do there.

9 Things I might **see**

   waves   boats   shells

10 Things I might **do**

   swim   sunbathe   paddle

PART B Focus
1–4: alternative spellings of the **long a** phoneme; rhyme
5: high-frequency words
6–8: using **them**, **then** and **they** in sentences, with capitals at start
9–10: choosing language specific to setting

C SENTENCE WORK

Complete the sentence.

1 _We like_   to play outside.
2 _My dad_   made cakes.
3 _Grandpa_   sat in the armchair.
4 _Sarah_   visited her friends.

5 What is wrong with this sentence? **There were three eggs. In the nest.**

   You don't need a full stop after eggs because it's not the end of the sentence.

6 Write it correctly.   _There were three eggs in the nest._

Write the sentence correctly.

7 The boy fell asleep. In the sun.   _The boy fell asleep in the sun._
8 Ben shouted. From the window.   _Ben shouted from the window._

Add a describing word.

9 They set off into the _dark_ wood.
10 Suddenly, they saw a _huge_ bear.

PART C Focus
1–4: ensuring that sentences make sense; using capitals correctly
5–8: sentence punctuation
9–10: adding descriptive words

X DEFINITIVE ANSWER   X SAMPLE ANSWER

Section 1 Test 3

A WARM-UP

Add the missing letters to make a new word.

1 t h e _r_ e   **2** t h e _s_ e

3 Make the words into a sentence.

an A insect bee is

A bee is an insect.

4 Write four words that rhyme with **see**.

b _ee_   t r _ee_   g l _ee_   m _e_

5 Which word is the odd one out and why?

'me', because it is spelt differently

6 Write four words that rhyme with **ate**.

l _ate_   p l _ate_   s k _ate_   w _ait_

7 Which word is the odd one out and why?

'wait', because it is spelt differently

Complete the sentence.

8 _The tiger_ ate all the food.

9 _The dog_ barked at the cat.

10 _The pirates_ found the gold.

PART A Focus
1–2: high-frequency words
3: sentence punctuation; use of a and an
4–7: rhymes; phonemes
8–10: ensuring that sentences begin with a capital letter and make sense

B WORD WORK

Add the letters to the correct word.

ow   oa   o

1 b _ow_ l

2 c _o_ l d

3 g _oa_ l

PART B Focus
1–6: spellings of the **long o** phoneme
7–8: spelling of verb ending **ing**
9–10: vocabulary choice and spelling of colours

Use the words in these sentences.

4 I am ___cold___ .

5 That was a great ___goal___ .

6 Put the eggs in a ___bowl___ .

These words are wrongly spelt.

pushin   pullin   jumpin

7 Why is the spelling wrong?

The words should have 'ing' on the end, not 'in'.

8 Write the three words correctly.

pushing   _pulling_   _jumping_

Add colour words.

9 Grapes can be ___green___ or ___purple___ .

10 A zebra has ___black___ and ___white___ stripes.

C SENTENCE WORK

Add a word so that the sentence makes sense.

1 Sam ___walked___ down the road.

2 The ___boy___ sat on the wall.

3 He lived in a ___huge___ house.

4 The ___wizard___ gave him a book.

Write a sentence using the two words in **bold**.

5 **boy**   **gate**   _The boy opened the gate._

6 **girl**   **tree**   _The girl sat under the tree._

7 **cat**   **playground**   _There was a cat in the playground._

Add full stops and capital letters.

8 <ins>W</ins>we go swimming on <ins>M</ins>monday.

9 <ins>M</ins>meet <ins>E</ins>ellie at four o'clock.

10 <ins>I</ins>i am in the garden. <ins>C</ins>come and find me.

PART C Focus
1–4: choosing the right type of word to make sentence make sense
5–7: writing complete sentences with correct punctuation
8–10: checking punctuation; uses of capital letters

X DEFINITIVE ANSWER   X SAMPLE ANSWER

Section 1 Test 4

A WARM-UP

1 Write three words that rhyme with **goat**.

boat   coat   float

Use the three letters to make a word.

2 e o t   _t o e_

3 e i p   _p i e_

4 t o u   _o u t_

Finish the sentence.

5 This little duck   _goes quack._

6 All ducks   _have feathers._

7 One day the ducks   _went for a swim._

The same letter is missing from all these words.
Write it in.

8 w _a_ s

9 h _a_ d

10 t _a_ k e

> **PART A Focus**
> **1:** rhyme; spelling of **long o** phonemes (check for alternative spellings)
> **2–4:** visual spelling skills
> **5–7:** sentence construction and punctuation; grammatical accuracy
> **8–10:** high-frequency words; visual spelling skills

B WORD WORK

Underline the correct spelling.

1 nite   <u>night</u>   niyt   niet

2 <u>time</u>   tighm   tiem   tyme

3 flie   fligh   <u>fly</u>   fliy

Add the second syllable.

4 sis _t e r_

5 chil _d r e n_

6 num _b e r_

> **PART B Focus**
> **1–3:** long i vowel phoneme
> **4–6:** syllables; high-frequency words
> **7:** alphabetical order
> **8–10:** spelling the verb ending ing

7 Write the words in alphabetical order.

children

number

sister

8 Add the **ing** ending.

float_ing_   splash_ing_   throw_ing_   catch_ing_

Use the words in these sentences.

9 I like _splashing_ and _floating_ in water.

10 We were _throwing_ and _catching_ the ball.

C SENTENCE WORK

1 Cross out the word **and** in this story.

the King lost his crown ~~and~~ he was very angry ~~and~~ everyone had to look for it

2 How many sentences are there now?   _three_

3 Write the story as separate sentences with full stops and capital letters.

The King lost his crown. He was very angry. Everyone had to look for it.

4 Write another sentence to go at the end of the story.

The Queen found it on his throne.

Finish the sentence.

5 The Prince was very   _shocked._

6 The man was very   _old._

7 The bear cub was very   _shy._

Cross out the word that is wrong. Write the correct word.

8 He fell ~~of~~ the swing.   _off_

9 He planted a row ~~off~~ sunflowers.   _of_

10 The lion is king ~~off~~ the animals.   _of_

> **PART C Focus**
> **1–4:** forming and punctuating simple sentences rather than using **and**
> **5–7:** using describing words correctly and for different effects
> **8–10:** of/off

X DEFINITIVE ANSWER   X SAMPLE ANSWER

Section 1 Test 5

A   WARM-UP

Make three words using these letters only.

t a e

1. e a t
2. a t e
3. t e a

> **PART A Focus**
> 1–3: visual spelling skills
> 4–6: high-frequency words
> 7–10: writing sentences that are complete, make sense and are correctly punctuated

Add the missing letters.

4. g o o d   **Clue:** not bad
5. f i r s t   **Clue:** not last
6. l i g h t   **Clue:** not dark

Write two sentences about dogs.

7. Some people keep dogs as pets.
8. Dogs like to go for walks.

Write two sentences about bears.

9. Some bears are brown.
10. You can see bears in some zoos.

B   WORD WORK

Add the missing letters to make words that rhyme with the word in **bold**.

o u e

1. **moon**   s o o n   J u n e   s p o o n
2. **blue**   c l u e   t r u e   z o o
3. **pool**   f o o l   st o o l   r u l e

Add the same vowel sound to make two words.

4. fr i g h t   5. br i g h t

Write the meaning of the word in **bold**.

6. The dog **hurried** into the forest.
   'hurried' means went quickly

7. The girl saw something **gleaming** in the sunshine.
   'gleaming' means shining

8. The boy **clung** to the rocks.
   'clung' means held on tightly

> **PART B Focus**
> 1–3: rhyme; vowel phonemes oo and u-e
> 4–5: vowel phoneme igh
> 6–8: defining the meaning of words
> 9–10: common spelling errors; high-frequency words

Cross out the word that is wrongly spelt. Write the correct spelling.

9. We had ~~sum~~ cake for tea.   some
10. I ~~haf~~ a pet dog and a cat.   have

C   SENTENCE WORK

There is a word missing from these sentences. Rewrite each sentence so that it makes sense.

1. Mrs Jenkins reads newspaper.   Mrs Jenkins reads the newspaper.
2. It was dark the woods.   It was dark in the woods.
3. The dog the cat.   The dog saw the cat.
4. Della into the playground.   Della ran into the playground.

Add the full stops and capital letters.

5. ~~b~~Ben and ~~a~~Amy came to play. ~~w~~We had a great time.
6. ~~i~~It was late. ~~t~~The sun had gone in.
7. ~~t~~The ladybird was red. ~~i~~It had black spots.

Write a sentence using the word in **bold**.

8. **ran**   Ellie ran home.
9. **jumped**   The horse jumped over the fence.
10. **swinging**   The monkey was swinging in the tree.

> **PART C Focus**
> 1–4: rereading to check for sense
> 5–7: identifying and demarcating the start and end of a sentence
> 8–10: writing sentences that are complete, make sense and are correctly punctuated

8

X DEFINITIVE ANSWER   X SAMPLE ANSWER

Section 1   Test 6

A   WARM-UP

1 Write a sentence using the words **car** and **tree**.

He parked the car by the tree.

Change the vowel phoneme to make a new word.

2 l o a f → l <u>e</u> <u>a</u> f   *Clue: it grows on a tree*

3 b e a k → b <u>o</u> <u>o</u> k   *Clue: you read it*

4 m o a n → m <u>e</u> <u>a</u> n   *Clue: not kind*

5 Underline the odd one out.

may   stay   <u>they</u>   way

6 Why is it the odd one out?

Because it ends with 'ey' not 'ay'.

Complete the sentence.

7 *The little boy* _____ stood by the sea.

8 *The monster* _____ lived in the cave.

9 *He was* _____ watching television.

10 *The farmer* _____ grows vegetables.

> **PART A Focus**
> **1:** sentence construction
> **2–4:** long vowel phonemes
> **5–6:** common and irregular spelling patterns
> **7–10:** writing sentences that are complete, make sense and are correctly punctuated

B   WORD WORK

The same vowel phoneme is missing from both the words below. Write it in.

1 jam j <u>a</u> r   **2** shooting s t <u>a</u> r

Add the missing letters.

e i o

3 p r <u>i</u> d e   **4** s l <u>o</u> p e

Look at these words.

calld   pulld   screamd

5 What is wrong with the spelling?

They need 'ed' on the end.

Write the words correctly.

6 *called* _____

7 *pulled* _____

8 *screamed* _____

> **PART B Focus**
> **1–2:** vowel phoneme ar
> **3–4:** long vowel phonemes; modifying e
> **5–8:** verb ending ed
> **9–10:** two-syllable words; topic words (lights)

Add the missing syllable.

Clue: they give us light

9 c a n <u>dle</u>   **10** l a n <u>tern</u>

C   SENTENCE WORK

Make a question.

1 *What* _____ is your name?

2 *How* _____ old are you?

3 *Where* _____ do you live?

4 *Who* _____ is your best friend?

Change two words in the sentence. Write the new sentence.

5 ~~Archie~~ lived in a ~~little~~ house.   *Maria lived in a new house.*

6 The little ~~boy~~ went into the ~~street~~.   *The little girl went into the garden.*

7 There was an old ~~book~~ on the ~~shelf~~.   *There was an old box on the table.*

Underline the word that does **not** need a capital letter.

8 amy   lucy   <u>only</u>   emily

9 monday   sunday   friday   <u>today</u>

10 luke   i   <u>me</u>   danny

> **PART C Focus**
> **1–4:** using and spelling question words; adding question marks
> **5–7:** sentence variation
> **8–10:** using capital letters

X DEFINITIVE ANSWER   X SAMPLE ANSWER   9

A   WARM-UP

Make the words into a sentence.

1   **was the angry King**

The King was angry.

2   **sad little frog looked the**

The little frog looked sad.

3   **had good man idea a the**

The man had a good idea.

Add the missing letters to make three words that rhyme.

a o e

4   g _o_ a l

5   s t r _o_ l l

6   h _o_ l _e_

PART A Focus
1–3: writing sentences that are complete, make sense and are correctly punctuated
4–6: rhyme; **long o** vowel phoneme
7–10: high-frequency words; visual spelling skills

Use the three letters to make a word.

o h w

7   w h _o_

8   h _o_ w

Add the same letter to each of these words to make two new words.

9   _w_ h e n

10   _w_ h a t

B   WORD WORK

Make four words using these phonemes only.

b k p t ar

1   bar

2   part

3   art

4   bark

Write the missing word.

5   happily ever   after

6   far, far   away

7   Underline the odd one out.

Once upon a time …

A long, long time ago …

<u>Today it is very …</u>

There was once …

PART B Focus
1–4: blending phonemes; the phoneme ar
5–8: story language
9–10: two-syllable words; high-frequency words

8   Why is it the odd one out?

Because all the others sound as though they are from a story.

Add the missing syllables.

9   Sun _day_   Mon _day_   Tues _day_

10   four _teen_   fif _teen_   six _teen_

C   SENTENCE WORK

Write the next sentence.

1   First we had PE in the hall. Then   we got changed.

2   Yesterday it rained. Today   it was dry.

3   Last week the children planted sunflowers. Now   they have to water them every day.

4   The children fed the chickens. After that   they went to see the lambs.

Put a full stop or question mark at the end of the sentence.

5   Where are we going _?_

6   We are going to be late _._

7   It is nearly four o'clock _._

8   Will we get there on time _?_

PART C Focus
1–4: linked sentences that pick up on original idea, fit the connective and are correctly punctuated
5–8: sentence punctuation; identifying questions
9–10: rereading to check for sense and errors

Cross out the word that is wrong. Write the correct word.

9   We ~~wet~~ to the zoo on Monday.   went

10   He must ~~of~~ lost his way.   have

X DEFINITIVE ANSWER   X SAMPLE ANSWER

Section 1 Test 8

A WARM-UP

Add the missing letters.

ou ow

1. br _o_ _w_ n
2. sh _o_ _u_ t
3. t _o_ _w_ n
4. gr _o_ _w_ l
5. l _o_ _u_ d
6. f _o_ _u_ n d

7. Make the words into a question.

the garden is that who in

Who is that in the garden?

Write three words that rhyme with the word in **bold**.

8. **rain**   _drain_   _main_   _chain_
9. **gate**   _late_   _crate_   _date_

10. Write four question words.

what

when

why

where

> **PART A Focus**
> **1–6:** alternative spelling of vowel phoneme **ow**
> **7:** forming questions that are correctly worded and punctuated
> **8–9:** rhyme; spelling of vowel phonemes
> **10:** high-frequency words

B WORD WORK

Which words have the same spelling pattern?

stood could good would

1. _stood_ and _good_
2. _could_ and _would_

> **PART B Focus**
> **1–4:** vowel phoneme long oo
> **5–7:** defining the meaning of words
> **8–10:** verb endings ing and ed

These words also have a long **oo** sound.
Add the vowel phoneme.

3. h _o_ _o_ k
4. sh _o_ _u_ l d

Write the meaning of the words in **bold**.

5. The letter had been **scrunched up** and thrown away.

   'scrunched up' means _screwed up_

6. Suddenly the ground began to **quake**.

   'quake' means _shake_

7. The people were **alarmed**.

   'alarmed' means _worried_

Cross out the word that is wrongly spelt.
Write the correct spelling.

8. We ~~playd~~ games.   _played_
9. I like ~~singin.~~   _singing_
10. Last night it ~~snowd.~~   _snowed_

C SENTENCE WORK

Josh has been out. Write four questions to ask him.

1. _Where have you been?_
2. _Who went with you?_
3. _What did you see?_
4. _When did you get back?_

Add a word that fits the sentence.

5. The dog _played_ in the pond.
6. Raindrops _splashed_ on the windows.
7. The animals _lived_ in the woods.

> **PART C Focus**
> **1–4:** forming questions that are relevant and correctly punctuated
> **5–7:** selecting and spelling verbs in sentences
> **8–10:** identifying sentences and using sentence punctuation

Cross out the word **and**. Write separate sentences.

8. the robot went crazy ~~and~~ it was rushing round the room

   The robot went crazy. It was rushing round the room.

9. Ben was lost in the wood ~~and~~ it was dark ~~and~~ he was scared

   Ben was lost in the wood. It was dark. He was scared.

10. he sat by the tree ~~and~~ something fell on his head ~~and~~ it was an acorn

    He sat by the tree. Something fell on his head. It was an acorn.

Section 1   Test 9

A   WARM-UP

Change the vowel phoneme to make a new word.

1 h o r s e → h <u>o</u> u s e   *Clue: live in it*

2 b o o t → b <u>o</u> a t   *Clue: sail it*

3 b i k e → b <u>o o</u> k   *Clue: read it*

4 Write a question using these words.

where bird

Where did you see the bird?

The same vowel phoneme is missing from both rhyming words. Write it in.

5 s w <u>e e</u> t   s l <u>e e</u> t

6 t <u>e a</u> m   s c r <u>e a</u> m

> **PART A Focus**
> **1–3:** vowel phonemes
> **4:** forming and punctuating questions
> **5-6:** rhyme; the vowel phonemes ee and ea
> **7–10:** sentence variation

Add different words to make four sentences.

7 The ___old lady___ stood by the ___bridge___ .

8 The ___teacher___ stood by the ___door___ .

9 The ___boy___ stood by the ___wall___ .

10 The ___horse___ stood by the ___fence___ .

B   WORD WORK

Add the correct vowel phoneme.

ou ow

1 d <u>o w</u> n

2 s h <u>o u</u> t

3 a b <u>o u</u> t

> **PART B Focus**
> **1–3:** alternative spelling of long vowel phonemes
> **4–9:** words with more than one syllable; topic words (parts of a house)
> **10:** adding s to make plurals

Add the second syllable.

Clue: parts of a house

4 w i n d <u>o w</u>

5 g u t t <u>e r</u>

6 b a l c <u>o n</u> y

Add to the correct sentence the words from questions 4 to 6.

7 Let's sit on the ___balcony___ .

8 A ___window___ is made of glass.

9 The rain runs into the ___gutter___ .

10 Write the sentence correctly.

We saw six car and two van.

We saw six cars and two vans.

C   SENTENCE WORK

1 Why are these labels not complete sentences?

Our computer   Class Three   Mrs Butler

Because a sentence has to tell you something.

Write each label as a complete sentence.

2 This is our computer.

3 We are Class Three.

4 Mrs Butler is our teacher.

Cross out the word that is wrong. Write the correct word.

5 ~~Were~~ are the cakes for tea?   Where

6 What are you ~~wait~~ for?   waiting

7 Why ~~saw~~ the bus late?   was

Put the capital letters into the sentence.

8 ~~m~~M olly told ~~p~~P olly and ~~p~~P olly told me.

9 ~~m~~M onday is ~~m~~M rs ~~m~~M agee's washing day.

10 ~~d~~D avid and ~~d~~D aisy went to help ~~m~~M r ~~j~~J ones.

> **PART C Focus**
> **1–4:** understanding of the term sentence
> **5–7:** checking for grammatical errors
> **8–10:** using capital letters for names and titles

X DEFINITIVE ANSWER   X SAMPLE ANSWER

Section 1 Test 10

A WARM-UP

Add the missing letters so that the words rhyme.

o e w

1 g r <u>o w</u>

2 t <u>o e</u>

3 s n <u>o w</u>

> **PART A Focus**
> **1–3:** rhyme; vowel phoneme **long o**
> **4–6:** rhyme; spelling patterns
> **7–9:** sentence construction; full stops
> **10:** two-syllable words

Write two words that rhyme with the word in **bold**.

4 **like**   bike   hike

5 **ice**   dice   slice

6 **name**   came   blame

Finish the sentence.

7 The bird flew out of   the window.

8 The girl peeped through   the door.

9 It was dark in   the cellar.

10 Add the second syllable.

n u m <u>b e r</u>

B WORD WORK

Add the correct vowel phoneme.

ar or

1 s t <u>a r</u> t   3 s p <u>a r</u> k

2 s p <u>o r</u> t   4 s c <u>o r</u> n

Write the meaning of the word in **bold**.

5 The fox had a **crafty** plan.

'crafty' means   sly

6 He saw three **speckled** hens.

'speckled' means   covered with spots

7 The other foxes were **impressed** with his idea.

'impressed' means   they thought it was clever

Write two more words to make a sound pattern like this.

> **PART B Focus**
> **1–4:** choosing phonemes
> **5–7:** inferring meaning; definitions
> **8–10:** alliteration

ten tired tigers

8 seven   silly   snakes

9 five   funny   frogs

10 two   tiny   toads

C SENTENCE WORK

Write a question to go with the answer.

1 What was the weather like?   Answer: It was sunny every day.

2 How many sides does a square have?   Answer: It has four sides.

3 When do you go back to school?   Answer: We go back to school on Tuesday.

4 Why did you come inside?   Answer: Because I was cold.

The beginnings and endings of these sentences are mixed up.

The baby cried   **in the trees.**
Birds were singing   **under the water.**
The frog dived   **in his pushchair.**

Write the sentences correctly.

5 The baby cried in his pushchair.

6 Birds were singing in the trees.

7 The frog dived under the water.

Check and correct the sentence.

8 I̲ saw a dragon. in the wood.

9 H̲e ran has fast has he could.

10 T̲he tide is go͜ing out.

> **PART C Focus**
> **1–4:** forming questions to fit answers; question marks
> **5–7:** adding phrases to sentences
> **8–10:** checking sentence punctuation; correcting grammatical errors

Section 1   Test 11

A   WARM-UP

Add the missing vowel phoneme.

Clue: colours

1 b r o w n   **3** p u r p l e

2 b l u e   **4** g r e e n

5 Write a question using these words.
present party

What present are you taking
to the party?

6 Underline the odd one out.

soon   fool   noon   good

7 Why is it the odd one out?

Because the 'oo' makes a
different sound.

Add a letter to make a new word.

8 h i s

9 g a s

10 f o u r

> **PART A Focus**
> **1–4:** high-frequency words; vowel phonemes
> **5:** writing questions
> **6–7:** vowel phonemes
> **8–10:** spelling high-frequency words

B   WORD WORK

Add the missing vowels.

a e i u

1 s c r a p e

2 t u b e

3 s l i m e

> **PART B Focus**
> **1–6:** long vowel phonemes; modifying e
> **7–9:** adding **ed** endings to verbs; common spelling errors
> **10:** story language

Use the words in these sentences.

4 Scrape the mud off your boots.

5 The snail left a trail of slime .

6 I need a tube of toothpaste.

Cross out the word that is wrongly spelt.
Write the correct spelling.

7 She jumpt off the wall.   jumped

8 He pusht the door.   pushed

9 They helpt the man.   helped

10 Underline the two phrases that sound like a story.

a great big enormous …

a bee is an insect …

all of a sudden …

C   SENTENCE WORK

Complete the question.

1 Who lives here ?

2 What did Nessie do ?

3 How do you do ?

4 Why is the sky blue ?

Add words to make a sentence.

5 A dog jumped over the wall.

6 The owl was hooting in the tree .

7 Mum gave me a biscuit .

There is a word missing from the sentence. Use / to show where the missing word goes. Then write the word.

8 A baby lion / called a cub.   is

9 A triangle is a shape / three sides.   with

10 Some cars can / over rough ground.   drive

> **PART C Focus**
> **1–4:** forming, spelling and punctuating questions
> **5–7:** making sentences make sense
> **8–10:** checking for errors

X DEFINITIVE ANSWER   X SAMPLE ANSWER

A WARM-UP

Add a describing word that starts with the same letter as the animal's name.

1	curly	caterpillars
2	funny	frogs
3	hungry	hedgehogs
4	beautiful	butterflies

Add the missing vowel phoneme.

5 n o r t h

6 s o u t h

7 e a s t

8 w e s t

> **PART A Focus**
> **1–4:** alliterative effect
> **5–8:** vowel phonemes; topic words (points of the compass)
> **9–10:** complete sentences

9 Put a tick by the sentence that is complete.

a sunny day

Today it is rainy. ✓

10 Why did you choose this one?

It has a capital letter and full stop.

B WORD WORK

Finish the missing word.

1 The boat was s a i l i n g across the sea.

2 A bird came s w o o p i n g down.

3 A leaf was f l o a t i n g on the water.

4 The lamb made a b l e a t i n g sound.

Add the missing syllables.

Clue: all have wheels

5 t r a c t o r

6 l o r r y

7 c a r a v a n

> **PART B Focus**
> **1–4:** reading for meaning; predicting words from clues; using **ing** endings
> **5–7:** syllables; topic words (vehicles)
> **8–10:** language choice: describing objects

Write three words to describe the object.

8	a balloon:	round	light	bouncy
9	a stone:	hard	smooth	heavy
10	a sponge:	soft	squashy	holey

C SENTENCE WORK

Write the next sentence. It should say what happened next.

1	Harry waited at the bus stop.	Soon the bus came down the road.
2	We played party games.	After that we had tea.
3	First they went to the shoe shop.	Next they went to buy a coat.

Add the word to the correct sentence. **gleaming wicked brave murky**

4 The _brave_ mouse spoke to the lion.

5 The _wicked_ wizard cast his spell.

6 There was a star _gleaming_ high in the sky.

7 Something moved in the _murky_ shadows.

Add capital letters, full stops and question marks.

8 Where are Sunita and Lucy going?

9 When was Queen Victoria born?

10 What was that? It was just a drop of rain.

> **PART C Focus**
> **1–3:** writing linked sentences that say what happened next
> **4–7:** adventurous language choices
> **8–10:** proofreading; punctuation

Remind the pupil to complete Section 1 of the Progress chart on page 46 of the workbook.

| X DEFINITIVE ANSWER | X SAMPLE ANSWER |

Schofield & Sims English Skills 1

Section 1 Writing task assessment sheet: My day out

Name		Class/Set
Teacher's name		Date

Sentence structure and punctuation

	Always/often	Sometimes	Never
Writing makes sense (e.g., no missing words)			
Writes in clear and separate sentences (rather than using **and ... and ... and**)			
Full stops mark ends of sentences			
Capital letters mark start of sentences			
Capital letters used for names and titles			
Capital letter used for **I**			
Question marks used for questions			

Composition and effect

Sounds like a recount of an event			
Opening introduces the event			
Events linked in a simple sequence			
Ideas or events developed over more than one sentence			
Word choice appropriate to content			

Spelling

CVC, CCVC, CVCC words are correct			
Plausible spelling of phonically regular words			
Correct spelling of long vowel phonemes (e.g., **ee** or **ea**)			
Phonically regular two-syllable words are correct			
Irregular high-frequency words are correct (e.g., **was**, **said**, **once**)			
s added to form plurals			
ed and **ing** endings added to regular verbs			

Writing task summary

Schofield & Sims English Skills 1

Section 1 Completed proofreading task: Mick meets an alien

Name	Class/Set
Teacher's name	Date

one day mick wet for a walk. then he came bak and the street lookt very
different. There wos aliens in the gardins. one littul alien wos jumpin up
and doun. mick sed hello. to the alien. the alien beept bak at him.

Proofreading corrections marked above words: O (one→One), M (mick→Mick), n (wet→went), T (then→Then), c (bak→back), e (streat→street), ed (lookt→looked), were (wos→were), e (gardins→gardens), O (one→One), le (littul→little), a (wos→was), g (jumpin→jumping), w (doun→down), M (mick→Mick), ai (sed→said), T (the→The), ed c (beept bak→beeped back)

Proofreading task summary

Section 1 tasks summary

From: **English Skills 1 Answers** by Carol Matchett (ISBN 978 07217 1181 2). Copyright © Schofield & Sims Ltd, 2011. Published by Schofield & Sims Ltd, Dogley Mill, Fenay Bridge, Huddersfield HD8 0NQ, UK (www.schofieldandsims.co.uk). **This page may be photocopied for use within your school or institution only.**

Section 2 Test 1

A   WARM-UP

Finish the sentence.

1 The angry man *shouted at the boy.*

2 The lonely boy *had no friends.*

3 The hungry girl *wanted her dinner.*

Add the missing vowel phonemes.

a e i

4 r *i* d e

5 l i *e*

6 t *a* i l

7 Write the words in alphabetical order.

lie

ride

tail

Add the missing letters.

Clue: *found in a story*

8 c h *a* r a c t e r

9 e v *e* n t s

10 e n d *i* n g

> **PART A Focus**
> 1–3: sentence construction and punctuation
> 4–6: vowel phonemes
> 7: alphabetical order
> 8–10: spelling; topic words (stories)

B   WORD WORK

Add the missing vowel phoneme.

or aw

1 p *a w*

2 t h *o r* n

Write the word as a plural.

3 *paws*

4 *thorns*

Use the words in these sentences.

5 A rose bush has *thorns* .

6 A mouse has tiny *paws* .

> **PART B Focus**
> 1–2: correct spelling of vowel phonemes
> 3–6: using s for plurals
> 7–8: compound words
> 9–10: meaning of compound words

Write the two smaller words that make the compound word.

7 greenhouse *green* *house*

8 weekend *week* *end*

Write the meaning of the word.

9 a 'greenhouse' is *a place where you grow plants*

10 'weekend' means *Saturday and Sunday*

C   SENTENCE WORK

Put a tick if the caption is a complete sentence. Put a cross if it is not.

1 Lots of flowers *X*

2 We had fun on the swings. *✓*

3 Playing ball games *X*

Write as a sentence one of the captions with a cross beside it.

4 *There are lots of flowers.*

A word is missing. Give two ideas for what it might be.

5 The boat *overturned* *sank* in the stormy sea.

6 The people *bowed* *sang* to the King.

7 The lion *roared* *snarled* at the other animals.

Add full stops, capital letters and question marks.

8 *W*who is that at the door? *I*it must be *J*jack.

9 *W*what is *E*emma doing out there? *S*she will get cold.

10 *T*there was something moving in the bushes. *W*what was it?

> **PART C Focus**
> 1–4: understanding the term **sentence**
> 5–7: checking sense; suggesting possible words
> 8–10: identifying sentences; sentence and question punctuation

Section 2   Test 2

A   WARM-UP

Finish the sentence.

1 Alex was feeling ___*sad.*___

2 Sophie wanted to ___*play outside.*___

Add vowel phonemes to make different words.

3 b _o_ _a_ t   **4** b _a_ _i_ t

5 Change one letter to make a new word.

s t i l e → _s_ _t_ _o_ _l_ _e_   **Clue:** *took*

Add the missing vowel phoneme.

Clue: *you wear them*

6 s c _a_ r f   **8** j _e_ _a_ n s

7 b _o_ _o_ t s   **9** c _o_ _a_ t

10 Write the words in alphabetical order.

___*boots*___

___*coat*___

___*jeans*___

___*scarf*___

PART A Focus
1–2: composing complete sentences
3–5: vowel phonemes; changing words
6–9: vowel phonemes; topic words (clothes)
10: alphabetical order

B   WORD WORK

1 What do you notice about the grapheme **ear**?

clear pear swear dear

___*It can make two different sounds.*___

2 Sort the words into two sets.

Set 1: ___*pear*___   ___*swear*___

Set 2: ___*dear*___   ___*clear*___

PART B Focus
1–2: comparing phonemes for **ear** grapheme
3–7: syllables; vocabulary
8–10: vocabulary

Write in the missing syllable.

3 c a r _p_ _e_ _t_   **Clue:** *on the floor*

4 c o l _l_ _e_ _c_ _t_   **Clue:** *bring together*

5 f o r _t_ _u_ _n_ _e_   **Clue:** *lots of money*

6 v a _n_ _i_ _s_ _h_   **Clue:** *disappear*

7 s t a r _v_ _i_ _n_ _g_   **Clue:** *very hungry*

Underline the two describing words.

8 There was once a <u>naughty</u> <u>little</u> goat.

9 Sita was <u>lonely</u> and <u>afraid</u>.

10 A <u>huge</u> rock fell into the <u>icy</u> water.

C   SENTENCE WORK

Complete the sentence.

1 She saw the ghost and ___*ran off screaming.*___

2 He went into the garden and ___*planted some flowers.*___

3 A bird sat in the tree and ___*began to sing.*___

Sad Sid is a character in a story. Write three questions about him.

4 *Where does he live?*

5 *What does he do?*

6 *Why is he sad?*

Write the missing word.

was were is are

7 I ___*was*___ pleased with my work last term.

8 Today the flowers ___*are*___ starting to open.

9 Harry ___*is*___ outside at the moment.

10 My friends ___*were*___ going to visit me yesterday.

PART C Focus
1–3: completing compound sentences, with logical follow-on and correct punctuation
4–6: forming questions; using question marks
7–10: grammatical agreement

X **DEFINITIVE ANSWER**   X **SAMPLE ANSWER**   **19**

Section 2 Test 3

A WARM-UP

Add the same letter to every word in the list to make three new words.

1 w h o   w h a t   w h e n

2 t h e m   t h e r e   t h e n

3 c a l l   c o l d   c a n n o t

Write two sentences about lions.

4 A lion is a wild animal.

5 Lions live in Africa.

Write two questions about lions.

6 What do lions eat?

7 Where can you see lions?

Add the missing letters.

Clue: found in a non-fiction book

8 i n d e x

9 c o n t e n t s

10 g l o s s a r y

> **PART A Focus**
> **1–3:** high-frequency words
> **4-5:** simple sentences; grammatical agreement
> **6–7:** using question words and question marks
> **8–10:** spelling of topic words (non-fiction)

B WORD WORK

Put the correct letters into each word.

ur er ir

1 f i r s t

2 t u r n

3 t e r m

> **PART B Focus**
> **1–6:** alternative spellings of vowel phoneme **er**
> **7–8:** compound words
> **9–10:** choice of appropriate verbs in past or present tense

Use the words in these sentences.

4 _____First_____ , beat the eggs.

5 See you next ____term____ .

6 Now it is my ____turn____ .

Use these words to make two compound words.

sun week day set

7 sunset   8 weekday

Write two words that you could use in this sentence.

The boy _____ across the playground.

9 ran   10 shouted

C SENTENCE WORK

Write the missing word.

1 Dogs ____are____ often kept as pets.

2 A sunflower ____is____ yellow.

3 For many years the people ____were____ happy.

4 The next day the frog ____was____ still there.

Finish the sentence.

5 The clock struck twelve and *everyone stopped.*

6 The clock struck twelve but *no-one noticed.*

7 Dan woke up and *looked around.*

8 Dan woke up but *it was still dark.*

9 What is wrong with this writing? **The house was old. And creepy.**

It should be one sentence.

10 Write it correctly.

The house was old and creepy.

> **PART C Focus**
> **1–4:** grammatical agreement; past and present tense (is/are, was/were)
> **5–8:** compound sentences; using **and** and **but**
> **9–10:** identifying sentences; sentence punctuation

X DEFINITIVE ANSWER   X SAMPLE ANSWER

A WARM-UP

Add the missing vowel phoneme.

or ar

1 c <u>o</u> r n

2 m <u>a</u> r k

3 f <u>o</u> r k

Complete the sentence.

4 *Dad was* _____ in the kitchen.

5 *The dog was* _____ in the garden.

Add the missing vowel phonemes to these compound words.

6 b <u>i</u> r t h d <u>a</u> y   **7** f <u>o</u> o t b <u>a</u> l l

Put the letters in order to make a word.

8 e n t w   *went*

9 r e h   *her*

10 a e h v   *have*

> **PART A Focus**
> **1–3:** blending phonemes
> **4–5:** sentence structure
> **6–7:** spelling vowel phonemes; compound words
> **8–10:** high-frequency words

B WORD WORK

1 What do you notice about these words?

chair	wear	care
square	bear	hair

They all rhyme.

Put together the words with the same spelling pattern.

2 *chair* and *hair*

3 *bear* and *wear*

4 *care* and *square*

> **PART B Focus**
> **1–4:** alternative spellings of the vowel phoneme **air**
> **5–6:** verb ending **ed**; common spelling errors
> **7–10:** vocabulary choice

Write correctly the word that is wrongly spelt.

5 They **startid** to scream.   *started*

6 He **liftid** up the frog.   *lifted*

Write four words you might use to describe a dragon.

7 *green*

8 *fierce*

9 *fiery*

10 *scaly*

C SENTENCE WORK

The beginnings and endings of these sentences are mixed up.

Some bears	**have fur.**
A polar bear	**are brown.**
All bears	**live in the Arctic.**
Polar bears	**is white.**

Write the sentences correctly.

1 *A polar bear is white.*

2 *All bears have fur.*

3 *Polar bears live in the Arctic.*

4 *Some bears are brown.*

Matt fell off the wall. Write three questions to ask about this event.

5 *Where did it happen?*

6 *How did it happen?*

7 *When did it happen?*

Write the missing word. **and but so**

8 They ran and ran ___*but*___ still the giant followed them.

9 The boy hid ___*and*___ waited to see what happened.

10 The door was open ___*so*___ she went inside.

> **PART C Focus**
> **1–4:** making sense; grammatical agreement
> **5–7:** forming relevant questions; using question marks
> **8–10:** connectives; compound sentences

[X] DEFINITIVE ANSWER   [X] SAMPLE ANSWER

21

Section 2 Test 5

A WARM-UP

Underline the correct spelling.

1 wer <u>wear</u> wayre wair

2 squer squear <u>square</u> squair

3 er <u>air</u> ayer aire

Add a rhyming word to make a question like this one.

Does a cow meow?

4 Does a snake <u>shake?</u>

5 Does a bear <u>glare?</u>

6 Does a sheep <u>weep?</u>

7 Does a crow <u>glow?</u>

Use these words to make three compound words.

bed door way motor room

8 <u>bedroom</u>

9 <u>doorway</u>

10 <u>motorway</u>

> **PART A Focus**
> **1–3:** spelling of phoneme **air**
> **4–7:** spelling rhyming words; choosing verbs; forming/ punctuating questions correctly
> **8–10:** compound words

B WORD WORK

Add the correct letters to these rhyming words.

1 z <u>o</u> o

2 t r <u>u</u> <u>e</u>

3 c h <u>e</u> <u>w</u>

Write another word that ends with this vowel phoneme.

4 <u>b</u> <u>l</u> e w

5 <u>c</u> <u>l</u> u e

Add **ful** or **ly** to make a new word.

6 soft <u>ly</u>   7 pain <u>ful</u>

Use the new word in a sentence.

8 The rain fell <u>softly</u> .

9 His leg was very <u>painful</u> .

10 Write the pair of opposites.

old gloomy new dull

<u>old</u> and <u>new</u>

> **PART B Focus**
> **1–5:** different spellings of **long oo** phoneme
> **6–9:** simple suffixes
> **10:** opposites

C SENTENCE WORK

Write a sentence with the three words in it.

1 **clown and laugh** The clown fell down and we started to laugh.

2 **tea but cup** I wanted some tea but there was no cup.

3 **house but door** We went to the house but the door was locked.

4 **lion when people** The people were frightened when they saw the lion.

Put the capital letters into the sentence.

5 on friday miss muffet went to see humpty dumpty.
   O F   M M   H   D

6 on saturday goldilocks went to see jack horner.
   O S   G   J H

7 on sunday everyone was tired. they all stayed at home.
   O S   T

Write the correct word.

Finally First Next

8 <u>First</u> , pour some cornflakes into a bowl.

9 <u>Next</u> , add some ice cold milk.

10 <u>Finally</u> , you can enjoy your breakfast.

> **PART C Focus**
> **1–4:** writing compound sentences that make sense and are correctly punctuated; using **and** and **but**
> **5–7:** capital letters for names, titles, days of the week and start of sentences
> **8–10:** using connectives to link sentences

X DEFINITIVE ANSWER   X SAMPLE ANSWER

Section 2   Test 6

A   WARM-UP

1   Underline the odd one out.

score   **wore**   <u>**floor**</u>   **tore**

2   Why is it the odd one out?

The ending is 'oor' not 'ore'.

A word is missing. Give two ideas for what it might be.

3   Ollie <u>*ate*</u> <u>*stole*</u> the cakes.

4   The gorilla <u>*sat*</u> <u>*swung*</u> in the tree.

5   The ghost <u>*floated*</u> <u>*flew*</u> around us.

Write the correct spelling.

6   shoutid <u>*shouted*</u>

7   jumpt <u>*jumped*</u>

8   growlin <u>*growling*</u>

> **PART A Focus**
> **1–2:** alternative spelling of vowel phonemes *or*
> **3–5:** making sense; vocabulary choice
> **6–8:** verb endings **ed** and **ing**
> **9–10:** simple sentences; questions with question marks

9   Write a sentence about popcorn.

I like popcorn very much.

10   Write a question about popcorn.

How do you make popcorn?

B   WORD WORK

Add the vowel phoneme, spelt correctly.

eer ear

1   c h <u>eer</u> f u l

2   c l <u>ear</u> l y

3   p <u>eer</u> i n g

> **PART B Focus**
> **1–6:** alternative spelling of vowel phonemes; simple suffixes
> **7–8:** compound words, correct spelling of vowel phonemes
> **9–10:** word definitions

Use the words in these sentences.

4   I saw it <u>*clearly*</u> .

5   Joe is always bright and <u>*cheerful*</u> .

6   She was <u>*peering*</u> at us.

Underline the correct spelling of these compound words.

7   upsters   upstares   <u>upstairs</u>

8   <u>doorstep</u>   dorstep   dorestep

Write the meaning of the word in **bold**.

9   A bus is **designed** to carry many people.

'designed' means *specially made*

10   The wheels are **attached** to the axle.

'attached' means *joined on*

C   SENTENCE WORK

The child went to her granny's house and there was no-one there.

1   Write two sentences instead of using **and**. *The child went to her granny's house. There was no-one there.*

2   Write the two sentences as one. Use the word **but**. *The child went to her granny's house but there was no-one there.*

3   Write the next sentence in the story. *She looked for her granny in the garden but there was no-one there.*

Write the missing word.   **eat catches bakes throw**

4   She <u>*bakes*</u> cakes.

5   They <u>*eat*</u> lots of cakes.

6   I <u>*throw*</u> the ball.

7   He <u>*catches*</u> the ball.

Add the punctuation and capital letters to these jokes.

8   ^W^what do you call a tiny bee? ^A^a babee.

9   ^W^what game do cows play? ^M^moosical chairs.

10   ^H^how do you start an insect race? ^O^one, two, flea, go.

> **PART C Focus**
> **1–3:** simple and compound sentences
> **4–7:** grammatical agreement; making sense
> **8–10:** full stops, capital letters and question marks

X DEFINITIVE ANSWER   X SAMPLE ANSWER

Section 2 Test 7

A WARM-UP

Add the same letter to all these words to make new words.

1. s c r a p _e_
2. c u b _e_
3. s l o p _e_

Write three words that rhyme with the word in **bold**.

4. **wave** _cave_ _gave_ _brave_
5. **round** _found_ _hound_ _ground_

Finish the sentence.

6. The box was open but _there was_ _nothing in it._
7. He shouted but _no-one came._
8. Emily was scared but _still went on._

Write in the missing syllable.

Clue: _found in a non-fiction book_

9. head _ing_ **Clue:** _at the top of a page_
10. cap _tion_ **Clue:** _goes with a picture_

B WORD WORK

Write a word that rhymes with the word in **bold**.

1. **boil** _coil_
2. **boy** _joy_
3. **join** _coin_

Underline the correct spelling.

4. takeing takin <u>taking</u> takking
5. <u>smiling</u> smileing smilling smilin
6. comeing comming comig <u>coming</u>

Add **un** or **dis** to make the opposite.

7. lucky and _unlucky_
8. agree and _disagree_

Add one of the words you have just made.

9. Tom and Megan sometimes _disagree_ .
10. The team was _unlucky_ in the match.

C SENTENCE WORK

Make a question.

1. _What are_ the five senses _?_
2. _Where is_ Stoke on the map _?_
3. _Who is_ the captain of the football team _?_
4. _Where are_ you going on holiday _?_

Make the sentence into two separate sentences.

5. He opened the door and went inside. ~~and~~ ^I^it was dark.
6. He returned home and gave the gold to his wife. ~~and~~ ^S^she was very happy.
7. It was late and starting to get dark. ~~and~~ ^T^they were still far from home.

Finish the sentence.

8. It was very hot outside so _we sat in the shade._
9. A tiger has escaped from the zoo so _we are looking out for it._
10. It is nearly bedtime so _I will go and brush my teeth._

X DEFINITIVE ANSWER   X SAMPLE ANSWER

Section 2　Test 8

A　WARM-UP

Add the same vowel phoneme to all these words.

1　m o_r n i n g　　s t o_r m　　f o_r k

2　Write two more words with this phoneme.

_____cork_____　and　_____sport_____

Write a sentence using these words.

3　**park but rain**

We met at the park but it began to rain.

4　**happy but sad**

Sam was happy but Jen was sad.

Add **un** or **dis** to make the opposite.

5　happy　_unhappy_

6　appear　_disappear_

7　selfish　_unselfish_

8　loved　_unloved_

9　honest　_dishonest_

> **PART A Focus**
> **1–2:** blending phonemes; the phoneme or
> **3–4:** compound sentences using **but**, with correct punctuation and linked meanings
> **5–9:** using **un** and **dis** to make opposites and negatives
> **10:** graphemes **ear** and **are**

10　Put the letters in order to make two words.

a e d r

_____dear_____　and　_____dare_____

B　WORD WORK

Underline the odd one out.

1　creak　sneak　<u>break</u>　beak

2　It is the odd one out because

it does not rhyme with the others.

3　<u>how</u>　snow　glow　throw

4　It is the odd one out because

it does not end with the same sound.

5　Write two words that rhyme with the answer to question 3.

_____now_____　and　_____cow_____

Add the vowel phonemes to the compound word.

6　f a_i r g r o_u n d

7　p a_i n t b r u_sh

8　a_r m c h a_i r

> **PART B Focus**
> **1–5:** different pronunciations of graphemes
> **6–8:** compound words; vowel phonemes
> **9–10:** opposites

Write an opposite for each of these words.

9　far　_near_

10　empty　_full_

C　SENTENCE WORK

Write the next sentence.

1　A snail is a small creature. _It has a hard shell._

2　Cows live on farms. _They give us milk._

3　Tim the tiger looked around. _He could not see his mum anywhere._

4　Sam and Sophie were scared. _They did not know what to do._

5　Which of the sentences sound like non-fiction? Tick the numbers.

1 ✓　　2 ✓　　3　　4

Add describing words to the sentence.

6　The _greedy_ girl ate all the _lovely_ cakes.

7　Jack was a _friendly_ boy with a _cheerful_ face.

Correct anything that is wrong.

8　~~Were~~ _Where_ is ~~mark~~ _Mark_? He ~~are~~ _is_ late.

9　We ~~was~~ _were_ going to see a show but it ~~were~~ _was_ sold out.

10　I ~~were~~ _was_ ill but now I ~~is~~ _am_ better.

> **PART C Focus**
> **1–5:** writing linked sentences (in fact and fiction style) that are correctly punctuated and follow on appropriately
> **6–7:** adding descriptive detail
> **8–10:** checking accuracy and punctuation

X DEFINITIVE ANSWER　　X SAMPLE ANSWER

Section 2   Test 9

A   WARM-UP

Use these words to make three compound words.

pop flake snow corn

1 popcorn

2 snowflake

3 cornflake

PART A Focus
1–3: compound words
4–7: ensuring that sentences make
sense; grammatical agreement; tense
8–10: vowel phonemes; blending

The beginnings and endings of these sentences are
mixed up.

An elephant	are tiny.
A mouse	were huge.
Ladybirds	is big.
Dinosaurs	is small.

Write the sentences correctly.

4 An elephant is big.

5 A mouse is small.

6 Ladybirds are tiny.

7 Dinosaurs were huge.

Add vowel phonemes to make different words.

8 m e a n   m o a n   m a i n

9 f e e l   f o a l   f o w l

10 t u r n   t o r n   t o w n

B   WORD WORK

Add the missing phonemes to the compound word.

1 f a r m y a r d

2 g o a l k e e p e r

Complete the word sum.

3 **hide** + **ing** = hiding

4 **make** + **ing** = making

Underline the describing word.

5 a ghastly monster

6 a wise man

7 a kind nurse

PART B Focus
1–2: compound words; correct
spelling of vowel phonemes
3–4: adding ing to verbs ending
with e
5–10: vocabulary; meaning of
words; opposites

Write each describing word next to its opposite.

8 cruel → kind

9 foolish → wise

10 lovely → ghastly

C   SENTENCE WORK

The magic rose is the title of a story.

Write five questions that the story might answer.

1 Who finds the magic rose?

2 Where do they find it?

3 When did the story take place?

4 What colour is the magic rose?

5 Why is the rose magic?

Finish the sentence in three different ways.

6 **The old man was tired so** he sat down to rest.

7 **The old man was tired but** he carried on working.

8 **The old man was tired and** wanted his lunch.

Underline the word that is wrong. Write the correct word.

9 We went to the zoo and see lots of animals.   saw

10 They raced across the sand and runs into the sea.   ran

PART C Focus
1–5: forming relevant questions
using question words and
question marks
6–8: forming compound
sentences that reflect the
connectives used (and, but, so)
9–10: maintaining past tense

26   X DEFINITIVE ANSWER   X SAMPLE ANSWER

Section 2 Test 10

A WARM-UP

Use these words to make three compound words.

card code board post

1. cardboard
2. postcode
3. postcard

Add the missing letters. **Clue:** *places*

4. s t r _e_ _e_ t
5. f _i_ e l d
6. s _e_ _a_ s i d e

> **PART A Focus**
> **1–3:** compound words
> **4–6:** correct spelling of vowel phonemes; topic words (places)
> **7–8:** compound sentences using **but**
> **9–10:** vocabulary choice; describing words

Complete the sentence.

7. ___I tried to get the jar___ but I could not reach it.

8. ___We wanted to go outside___ but it was too cold.

Write two words to describe the sun.

9. hot   10. powerful

B WORD WORK

Underline the correct spelling.

1. neerly   <u>nearly</u>   nerely   nearley
2. hert   hirt   <u>hurt</u>   herrt

Write in the missing syllable.

3. p o w _e r_ f u l
4. f o r _g e t_ f u l
5. h a p p _i_ l y

> **PART B Focus**
> **1–5:** using knowledge of phonemes and suffixes
> **6–8:** using suffixes; word meanings
> **9–10:** inferring meaning

Use each word in one of these sentences.

6. They all lived ___happily___ ever after.
7. The magic was very ___powerful___ .
8. Jack was very ___forgetful___ .

Write the meaning of the word in **bold**.

9. Many houses were **destroyed** in the fire.
   'destroyed' means ___damaged or ruined___

10. The castle is now a **ruin**.
    a 'ruin' is ___the damaged part that is left when everything else is destroyed___

C SENTENCE WORK

Finish the sentences to continue the story.

1. They set off to find the palace. Before long ___they reached a river.___
2. Then they had to go up a steep hill. After a long time, ___they saw it in the distance.___
3. At last they reached the palace gates. Suddenly, ___an old woman appeared.___

Read the sentence. Write a word that is the opposite of the word in **bold**.

4. He lived in a **tiny** house.   gigantic
5. The animals were **pleased**.   disappointed
6. It was a **sunny** day.   cloudy
7. The King was **kind**.   cruel

> **PART C Focus**
> **1–3:** using connectives to link events or sentences in a plausible way
> **4–7:** opposites; descriptive words
> **8–10:** changing verbs to past tense

Write the sentence as if the event has already happened.

8. They play in the garden. On Saturday ___they played in the garden.___
9. It is cold. Last night ___it was cold.___
10. Joe has three stickers. Last week Joe ___had three stickers.___

Section 2 Test 11

A WARM-UP

Add the second syllable. **Clue:** *all pets*

1 h a m <u>s t e r</u>
2 r a b <u>b i t</u>
3 g o l d <u>f i s h</u>

4 Write the words in alphabetical order.

<u>goldfish</u>   <u>hamster</u>   <u>rabbit</u>

Change two words. Write the new sentence.

5 The old ~~man~~ was ~~clever.~~

The old woman was foolish.

6 The ~~path~~ led to a little ~~cottage.~~

The steps led to a little doorway.

7 There was a tall ~~tree~~ by the ~~fence.~~

There was a tall man by the river.

Add a vowel phoneme to complete the word.

8 n <u>o o</u> n
9 s n <u>o</u> w
10 d <u>a</u> y

> **PART A Focus**
> **1–3:** spelling two-syllable words
> **4:** alphabetical order
> **5–7:** sentence variation
> **8–10:** vowel phonemes

B WORD WORK

1 Complete this list of rhyming words.

roar   d <u>o o</u> r   f <u>o r</u>   m <u>o r e</u>

2 What do you notice about the words?

They have different spellings.

Add **un** or **dis** to make the opposite.

3 <u>un</u> s a f e
4 <u>dis</u> o b e y
5 <u>un</u> l o c k

Use the words in these sentences.

6 He could not ___*disobey*___ .

7 The teacher will ___*unlock*___ the room.

8 That wall is ___*unsafe*___ .

> **PART B Focus**
> **1–2:** different spellings of vowel phoneme or
> **3–8:** understanding common prefixes
> **9–10:** identifying syllables

Add the missing syllable.

9 r u b <u>bish</u>   **Clue:** *junk*

10 h a i r <u>dress</u> e r   **Clue:** *cuts hair*

C SENTENCE WORK

A word is missing. Give two ideas for what it might be.

1 The children opened the door and ___*ran*___ ___*sped*___ into the street.

2 The man ___*fell*___ ___*jumped*___ down the stairs.

3 The dog ___*growled*___ ___*yapped*___ at the postman.

4 Snowflakes ___*drifted*___ ___*floated*___ to the ground.

Complete the sentence.

5 *They hurried on* _____ but it was getting late.

6 *Jack wanted to sell the cow* _____ so off he went to market.

7 *He ran to the river* _____ and jumped into the water.

Add punctuation and capital letters to these stories.

8 <u>J</u>jack and <u>J</u>jill were playing tennis. <u>T</u>tom wanted to join in.

9 <u>T</u>the bird saw the open window. <u>I</u>it flew into <u>M</u>mr <u>B</u>brown's house.

10 <u>T</u>the fox jumped out. <u>T</u>the children screamed and ran away.

> **PART C Focus**
> **1–4:** making sense; vocabulary choice
> **5–7:** compound sentences; using and, so, but with appropriate sentence openings
> **8–10:** using correct punctuation; identifying where sentences start/end

28

Section 2 Test 12

A WARM-UP

Change the vowel phoneme to make a new word.

1 f e e l → f <u>o i</u> l **Clue:** *silver paper*

2 l e a d → l <u>o u</u> d **Clue:** *not quiet*

3 b o r n → b <u>a</u> r n **Clue:** *has hay in it*

4 s o i l → s <u>a i</u> l **Clue:** *found on a boat*

Write a sentence to say what happened next.

5 Harry hid behind the tree.

He waited and watched.

6 The rabbit hopped away.

He was looking for food.

7 It began to rain.

I put up my umbrella.

> **PART A Focus**
> **1–4:** vowel phonemes
> **5–7:** writing linked but separate sentences, correctly punctuated
> **8–10:** rhyme; phonemes

Write three words that rhyme with the word in **bold**.

8 **park** *dark* *shark* *spark*

9 **corn** *torn* *dawn* *yawn*

10 **race** *place* *lace* *ace*

B WORD WORK

Add the missing letters to the compound word.

1 b r a i n <u>s t o r m</u> **Clue:** *think of ideas*

2 h i g h <u>l i g h t</u> **Clue:** *make it show up*

3 l a w n <u>m o w e r</u> **Clue:** *cuts the lawn*

Cross out the word that is wrongly spelt.
Write the correct spelling.

4 He was ~~liveing~~ here. *living*

5 They were ~~haveing~~ a party. *having*

6 I am ~~takeing~~ the bag to school. *taking*

Write the meaning of the words in **bold**.

7 The giant **approached** the village.
'approached' means *came close to*

8 His footsteps made the trees **tremble**.
'tremble' means *shake*

9 He **trampled on** Mrs Neil's roses.
'trampled on' means *trod on or flattened*

10 "I'm hungry," he **bellowed**.
'bellowed' means *shouted or roared*

> **PART B Focus**
> **1–3:** compound words; word meanings; spelling of phonemes
> **4–6:** adding ing to verbs ending with e
> **7–10:** working out meaning; vocabulary extension

C SENTENCE WORK

Continue these sentences so that they sound like a story.

1 Long ago there lived a *young boy called Jack.*

2 Far, far away stood a *glittering palace.*

3 Suddenly, there was a *loud noise.*

Cross out the words that describe the character. Add words that mean the opposite.

4 Joe was a ~~grumpy old~~ man. *cheerful* *young*

5 Ruby was a ~~rich young~~ lady. *poor* *old*

6 Ben was a ~~sad~~ and ~~quiet~~ child. *happy* *noisy*

7 The Prince was ~~poor~~ but ~~generous~~. *rich* *mean*

> **PART C Focus**
> **1–3:** using story language; sentence construction
> **4–7:** identifying words that describe; choosing antonyms
> **8–10:** understanding the purpose of speech marks

Finish the sentence.

8 "I will gobble you up," *said the monster.*

9 "I give you one wish," *said the wizard.*

10 "You are kind," *said the beggar.*

Remind the pupil to complete Section 2 of the Progress chart on page 46 of the workbook.

X DEFINITIVE ANSWER   X SAMPLE ANSWER

29

Schofield & Sims English Skills 1

Section 2 Writing task assessment sheet: Millie and the magic cooking pot

Name		Class/Set	
Teacher's name		Date	

Sentence structure and punctuation

	Always/often	Sometimes	Never
Writes in clear and separate sentences (rather than using **and** … **and** … **and**)			
Uses compound as well as simple sentences			
Uses simple connectives (**and**, **but**, **so**)			
Full stops mark end of sentences			
Capital letters mark start of sentences			
Capital letters used for names, titles, days of week, months of year			
Capital letter used for **I**			
Question marks used for questions			
Sentences grammatically accurate; correct use of singular and plural (e.g., **was/were**)			
Maintains use of past or present tense			

Composition and effect

Sounds like a story			
Has a beginning, middle and end			
Uses time-related words to sequence events			
Events expanded on (e.g., linked sentences include some detail)			
Uses story language			
Uses interesting vocabulary			

Spelling

Plausible spelling of phonically regular words			
Correct spelling of long vowel phonemes in familiar words including trigraphs			
Phonically regular compound and two-syllable words are correct			
Spelling of prefixes (**un** and **dis**) and suffixes (**ful** and **ly**) is correct			
Irregular high-frequency words are correct (e.g., **was**, **said**, **once**)			
s added to form plurals			
ed and **ing** endings added to verbs, including those with split digraphs (e.g., **joking**)			

Writing task summary

*From: **English Skills 1 Answers** by Carol Matchett (ISBN 978 07217 1181 2). Copyright © Schofield & Sims Ltd, 2011. Published by Schofield & Sims Ltd, Dogley Mill, Fenay Bridge, Huddersfield HD8 0NQ, UK (www.schofieldandsims.co.uk). **This page may be photocopied for use within your school or institution only.***

Schofield & Sims English Skills 1

Section 2 Completed proofreading task: Letter to Jack

Name	Class/Set
Teacher's name	Date

Deer jack, *(a J)*

Thank you for comeing to see me on my burthday. i hop you liket my jiant cake. *(i I e d g)*
And my jiant pizza. we was verry happy to see you. *(a g W were)*

i hope you find the gold coyn usefull. we did haf sum gold egg, but the chiken *(I i W ve some s c)*
keeps hideing them.

it is mrs large's buthday in june. we is going to haf a picnic. will you come and *(I M L ir J W are ve W)*
joyn us for thet? *(i a)*

Wiv best wishis, *(th e)*

jim large *(J L)*

Proofreading task summary

Section 2 tasks summary

Section 3 Test 1

Add the missing letters. **Clue: months**

1 M a r c h

2 J u n e

3 M a y

4 A u g u s t

Josie screamed. Write three questions about this event.

5 Who is Josie?

6 Why did she scream?

7 Where did she scream?

Change the vowel phoneme to make a new word.

8 t i m e → t a m e

Clue: not wild

9 w e e d → w o o d

Clue: comes from trees

PART A Focus
1–4: spelling high-frequency words
5–7: forming relevant questions using question words and question marks
8–10: vowel phonemes

10 s e e n → s o o n

Clue: in a short time

1 Add the missing letters.

ou oo ay

b o o k   g r o u n d

pl a y   c o o k

Put the words together to make two compound words.

2 playground   **3** cookbook

Write the meaning of the words in **bold**.

4 The powerful rocket will go to a **distant** planet.

'distant' means far away

Everyone hoped that the **fierce** animal would be **drowsy**.

5 'fierce' means wild and dangerous

6 'drowsy' means sleepy

Write the opposite.

7	powerful	weak
8	distant	near
9	fierce	gentle
10	drowsy	wide awake

PART B Focus
1: using vowel phonemes
2–3: compound words
4–6: working out meaning
7–10: opposites

Continue the sentence.

1 I stood on a chair so I could see.

2 She forgot her lunch so she was hungry.

3 There is a zebra crossing so we can cross safely.

4 A cup has a handle so you can hold it easily.

Cross out the describing words. Write words that mean the opposite.

5 The room was ~~bright~~ and ~~cheerful.~~   dull   gloomy

6 The land was ~~cold~~ and ~~damp.~~   hot   dry

7 He lived in a ~~tiny old~~ house.   huge   new

The capital letters in the sentence are mixed up. Make them correct.

8 Lucy's ~~B~~birthday is in ~~a~~April and ~~M~~mine is in ~~j~~July.

9 ~~I~~I went to Luke's ~~H~~house on ~~s~~Saturday. ~~h~~He came here on ~~s~~Sunday.

10 I was in ~~m~~Mrs ~~n~~Neil's ~~C~~class ~~L~~last ~~Y~~year ~~B~~but now ~~i~~I am in ~~m~~Mr ~~o~~Owen's.

PART C Focus
1–4: compound sentences using **so**, showing cause and effect
5–7: choosing describing words; antonyms
8–10: using capital letters

X DEFINITIVE ANSWER   X SAMPLE ANSWER

Section 3   Test 2

Add the missing letter.

o i a

1 n <u>a</u> m e

2 h <u>o</u> m e

3 f <u>i</u> n e

> **PART A Focus**
> **1–3:** vowel phonemes
> **4–5:** rhyme; spelling
> **6–7:** correct spelling
> **8–10:** using **so**, **but**, **and** to introduce a result, contrast or further information

Add a word. It should rhyme with the word in **bold**.

4 This **goat** has a ____*coat*____ .

5 This **whale** has a ____*tail*____ .

Underline the correct spelling.

6 werk   <u>work</u>   wurk   wirk

7 theef   theaf   <u>thief</u>   thefe

Finish this sentence in different ways.

8 Now they were rich so
they did not have to work.

9 Now they were rich but
they were not happy.

10 Now they were rich and
lived in a big house.

B   WORD WORK

1 Make eight words using these phonemes only.

sh m s c ore are

shore	*more*	*core*	*sore*
share	*mare*	*care*	*scare*

Write one more word with this phoneme.

2 **ore**   *snore*

3 **are**   *glare*

> **PART B Focus**
> **1–3:** blending vowel phonemes
> **4–7:** verb ending **ed**
> **8–10:** opposites

Add the correct word ending.

4 She went to the door and knock *ed* twice.

5 The room was empty so she walk *ed* in.

6 She saw the food and lick *ed* her lips.

7 Suddenly out jump *ed* a kitten.

Write the missing opposite.

8 People came from far and ____*near*____ .

9 The street was full of people,
young and ____*old*____ .

10 Meena has an old car and a ____*new*____ one.

C   SENTENCE WORK

Finish the second sentence.

1 The girl ran along the path. Meanwhile *the wolf was watching her.*

2 The old man went to bed. That night *there was a terrible storm.*

3 The lion lay down under the tree. Before long *he fell fast asleep.*

Add the correct word.

of have off

4 He must ____*have*____ left his bag at work.

5 There were lots ____*of*____ people in the street.

6 He should ____*have*____ switched ____*off*____ the lights.

7 The wind lifted the tent ____*off*____ the ground.

Add the full stops and capital letters.

8 We saw a snail. it had a shell. it moved very slowly.

9 Some old toys are clockwork. you need a key to wind them up.

10 The castle is very old. it was built on a hill so it was safe.

> **PART C Focus**
> **1–3:** using connectives to link sentences and continue ideas
> **4–7:** common errors
> **8–10:** marking sentence boundaries

Section 3   Test 3

A   WARM-UP

Change the vowel phoneme to make a new word.

1   s h o o k → s h <u>a</u> r k
2   w a d e → w <u>i</u> d e
3   s p e a k → s p <u>a</u> r k

Add two words to complete the sentence.

4   The <u>little</u> dog ran into the <u>dark</u> cave.
5   The <u>old</u> lady drove a <u>rusty</u> car.
6   A football is <u>round</u> and <u>bouncy</u>.

7   Underline the word that does **not** usually need a capital letter.

July   <u>Snowy</u>   Sunday   Amy

Add the missing letters.
Clue: *parts of a plant*

8   r <u>o</u> <u>o</u> t
9   l e <u>a</u> f
10 f l <u>o</u> <u>w</u> e r

> **PART A Focus**
> **1–3:** blending phonemes
> **4–6:** using adjectives in sentences
> **7:** capital letters
> **8–10:** vowel phonemes; topic words (plants)

B   WORD WORK

Write these words as two lists of rhyming words.

know slow how cow show now

1   <u>know</u>   <u>slow</u>   <u>show</u>
2   <u>how</u>   <u>cow</u>   <u>now</u>

Cross out the wrongly spelt words. Write the correct spellings.

3   She ~~startid~~ to ~~showt~~.
    <u>started</u>   <u>shout</u>

4   He ~~waitid~~ for the sun to ~~cum~~ out.
    <u>waited</u>   <u>come</u>

5   ~~Thay plantid~~ three trees.
    <u>They</u>   <u>planted</u>

> **PART B Focus**
> **1–2:** same spelling, different sounds
> **3–5:** common spelling errors
> **6–10:** synonyms; word meanings

Draw a line to join the words that have the same meaning.

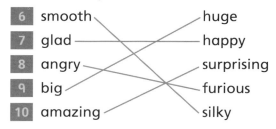

6   smooth   huge
7   glad   happy
8   angry   surprising
9   big   furious
10 amazing   silky

C   SENTENCE WORK

Finish the sentence.

1   A mango is sweet but lemons <u>are sour.</u>
2   Ants have six legs but a spider <u>has eight.</u>
3   Bicycles have two wheels but a tricycle <u>has three.</u>
4   Some eggs are brown but <u>others are white.</u>

Use the sentence to write a **why** question.

5   Sita started to cry.   <u>Why did Sita start to cry?</u>
6   The ground began to shake.   <u>Why did the ground begin to shake?</u>
7   Danny suddenly stopped talking. <u>Why did Danny suddenly stop talking?</u>

Cross out the word that does not make sense. Write the correct word.

8   He picked it up and ~~taked~~ it inside.   <u>took</u>
9   She found the pot and ~~maked~~ the tea.   <u>made</u>
10 It was dark when he ~~goed~~ home.   <u>went</u>

> **PART C Focus**
> **1–4:** compound sentences using **but** to show a contrast; grammatical agreement
> **5–7:** forming why questions; adding question marks
> **8–10:** irregular past tense

X DEFINITIVE ANSWER   X SAMPLE ANSWER

Section 3   Test 4

A   WARM-UP

Write three words that rhyme with the word in **bold**.

1 brown   down   town   clown

2 clout   shout   spout   out

Write two sentences about clouds.

3 Some clouds are white and fluffy.

4 Sometimes clouds bring rain.

Write two questions about clouds.

5 What are clouds made from?

6 Why are some clouds grey
and others white?

Write the opposite.

7 push   pull

8 open   close

9 good   bad

> **PART A Focus**
> **1–2:** rhyme; vowel phonemes
> **3–6:** forming sentences; questions that make sense and are correctly punctuated
> **7–9:** identifying opposites
> **10:** blending phonemes

10 Make five words using these phonemes only.

m n r l ai

main   mail   nail

rain   rail

B   WORD WORK

Add **ful** or **ly** to make a new word.

1 c a r e ful   **3** f r i e n d ly

2 l o n e ly   **4** t e a r ful

Add one of these new words to the sentence.

5 Everyone was very   friendly
at the new school.

6 Be   careful   not to break it.

7 The   lonely   little boy looked
sad and   tearful   .

> **PART B Focus**
> **1–4:** common suffixes
> **5–7:** common suffixes; word meanings
> **8–9:** common spelling patterns
> **10:** synonyms; word meanings

Write two words with the same spelling pattern as the word in **bold**.

8 fall   hall   small

9 fight   might   bright

Write one of these words instead of the words in **bold**. Check that it makes sense.

reach noticed return

10 He must **go back** home at once.   return

C   SENTENCE WORK

Finish the sentence.

1 He would have to hurry or he would be too late.

2 She had to find somewhere to hide or the robber would see her.

3 Always use suncream or you might get burned.

Add the commas.

4 At the farm we saw cows, sheep, pigs and chickens.

5 I like beans, carrots, peas and broccoli.

6 I had ham, cheese, peppers and mushrooms on my pizza.

7 Why are the commas needed?   To separate the items in a list.

> **PART C Focus**
> **1–3:** extending sentences using or and punctuating them correctly
> **4–7:** using commas in a list
> **8–10:** using connectives to link sentences

Add a word or phrase to link the two sentences.

8 They started to climb.   Eventually   they reached the top.

9 They went to sleep feeling happy.   The next morning   they woke early.

10 He began to clean the lamp.   Suddenly   there was a flash of light.

Section 3   Test 5

A   WARM-UP

1 Underline the odd one out.

moon   hoop   <u>wood</u>   food

2 Why is it the odd one out?

Because the 'oo' makes a
different sound.

Write a word that rhymes with the word in **bold**.

3 **moon**   *spoon*

4 **hoop**   *loop*

Finish the sentence.

5 Today it is very hot but *tomorrow it*
might rain.

6 Today it is very hot and *there is not*
much breeze.

7 Today it is very hot so *we are going*
to play in the paddling pool.

Add the missing vowel phoneme.

Clue: things that you write

8 r e p _o_ r t

9 r e c _o_ u n t

10 r h _y_ m e

B   WORD WORK

1 Make eight words using these letters only.

c h s t air ar

cars   *hair*   *chairs*   *tar*

stair   *star*   *art*   *arch*

Write one more word with this vowel phoneme.

2 **air**   *lair*   **3** **ar**   *card*

Write the word in **bold** using the correct prefix.

4 tidy and **intidy**   *untidy*

5 honest and **unhonest**   *dishonest*

6 known and **disknown**   *unknown*

7 visible and **unvisible**   *invisible*

Write the meaning of the words in **bold**.

All the plants had **withered** and died, **except for** one. This plant is now tall and **sturdy**.

8 'withered' means   *shrivelled up*

9 'except for' means   *apart from*

10 'sturdy' means   *strong*

C   SENTENCE WORK

Use these notes to help you write three sentences for the start of a story.

Jacob – farmer   **tiny cottage**   **lucky coin**

1 *There was once a farmer called Jacob.*

2 *He lived in a tiny cottage.*

3 *One day he found a lucky coin.*

Write the missing word.

his her our their

4 The lady put _her_ bag on the floor.

5 The boys told the teacher _their_ story.

6 Josh spoke to _his_ friend.

7 We wrote _our_ names at the top.

Add capital letters and punctuation.

8 Write the address on the envelope. ^Sstick a stamp on it. ^Pput the letter in a post box.

9 Do you like chocolate? ^Llots of people do. ^Wwhere does chocolate come from?

10 There were once three rabbits called ^Rrobbie, ^Bbobby and ^Rruby.

X DEFINITIVE ANSWER   X SAMPLE ANSWER

Section 3   Test 6

A   WARM-UP

1 Make six words using these letters only.

h n t ea ear

heat   hear   near

neat   tear   eat

PART A Focus
1: blending phonemes
2: forming compound sentences
3–6: compound words
7–10: choosing words to describe characters

2 Write a sentence using these words.

play but ball

We started to play but lost the ball.

These compound words have been mixed up. Write them correctly.

crosscase   spacebrush   hairship   bookword

3 crossword   **5** hairbrush

4 spaceship   **6** bookcase

Write a word that describes the character.

7 There was once a _poor_ fisherman.

8 There was once a _powerful_ king.

9 There was once a _lazy_ farmer.

10 There was once a _rich_ lady.

B   WORD WORK

Add the missing vowel.

a i o

1 s l i d e

2 h o p e

3 a m a z e

PART B Focus
1–3: vowel phonemes; modifying e
4–6: adding ing to verbs ending with e
7–8: spelling two- and three-syllable words
9–10: word meanings; synonyms

Add **ing** to the words you have made.

4 s l iding

5 h oping

6 a mazing

Add the missing syllable.   ***Clue:** both animals*

7 t i g e r

8 c r o c o d i l e

Write a word with the same meaning as the word in **bold**.

9 The food has gone **bad**.   rotten

10 It was a **cold** day.   chilly

C   SENTENCE WORK

1 Make the words into a sentence.

play can football you

You can play football.

2 Make the words into a question.

Can you play football?

3 Make the words into a sentence.

found have answer you the

You have found the answer.

4 Make the words into a question.

Have you found the answer?

PART C Focus
1–4: forming sentences; reordering words to make questions; adding appropriate punctuation
5–8: using a and an
9–10: using commas

Add **a** or **an**.

5 I had an apple, a banana and some grapes.

6 We saw an elephant, a lion and some baboons.

7 In my bag I had a balloon, an animal game, a pen and some sweets.

8 There was an oak tree a birch a willow and an elm.

9 What else is missing from the list of trees? The commas are missing.

10 Write the sentence correctly. There was an oak tree, a birch, a willow and an elm.

Section 3   Test 7

A WARM-UP

1 Write two words using these letters only.

e e h r t

three   there

> **PART A Focus**
> **1:** high-frequency words
> **2–4:** forming complete sentences with correct punctuation; adding an extra part
> **5–6:** vowel phonemes
> **7–10:** spelling regular two-syllable words; word meanings

Complete the sentence.

2 The dog growled and _ran to the gate._

3 The wise owl looked _down from the tree._

4 _The children were playing_ in the garden.

Add the missing letter.

i o u

5 b u r s t   s i r   w o r d

6 c u b e   k i t e   r o b e

Add the missing syllable.

7 b e g i n   *Clue: start*

8 f i n i s h   *Clue: end*

9 s u b t r a c t   *Clue: take away*

10 s e c o n d   *Clue: not first*

B WORD WORK

1 Underline the correct spelling.

foxis   foxs   <u>foxes</u>   foxxes

Make the words in **bold** into plurals.

2 We sell **clock** s and **watch** es .

3 Wash all the **plate** s and **dish** es .

4 Pack up the **case** s and **box** es .

Add the missing letters.

Clue: animal noises

5 g r o w l

6 b a r k

7 s n a r l

> **PART B Focus**
> **1–4:** adding s or es to make plurals
> **5–7:** vowel phonemes
> **8–10:** using synonyms for high-frequency words

Write one of these words instead of the word crossed out.

recognised seized offered

8 They ~~knew~~ _recognised_ him at once.

9 They ~~gave~~ _offered_ him a drink.

10 He ~~got~~ _seized_ the rope.

C SENTENCE WORK

Finish the sentence.

1 The boy asked for more bread because _he was hungry._

2 Jade trusted the old lady because _she seemed kind._

3 The sun looks small because _it is so far away._

4 Some people go jogging because _they want to get fit._

Write the missing words.

5 A _strange_ _little_ man waited by the _wooden_ door.

6 She was wearing a _straw_ hat with _yellow_ flowers.

7 The _fluffy_ _little_ puppy lay by the _blazing_ fire.

> **PART C Focus**
> **1–4:** sentence structure; using because to show cause and effect
> **5–7:** adding descriptive detail
> **8–10:** identifying and punctuating sentence boundaries

Add the full stops and capital letters.

8 He ran and ran and ran. Finally he stopped. He could run no more.

9 Lucy saw a lion. The lion saw Lucy. The lion roared and Lucy ran away.

10 In July it is often hot and sunny. In January it is much colder.

X DEFINITIVE ANSWER   X SAMPLE ANSWER

Section 3 Test 8

A WARM-UP

Change the vowel phoneme to make a new word.

1. g l o o m → g l e a m   *Clue: shine*
2. b u r s t → b o a s t   *Clue: show off*
3. s p o o k → s p a r k   *Clue: tiny light*
4. f i r s t → f e a s t   *Clue: big meal*
5. t u r n → t o r n   *Clue: ripped*

Both words have the same letters missing.
Write them in.

6. o v e r   a f t e r
7. w o u l d   s h o u l d

> **PART A Focus**
> 1–5: vowel phonemes; word meanings
> 6–7: common spelling patterns
> 8–10: using connectives to form longer sentences; adding a clause; capital letters

Complete the sentence.

8. _She tried the soup_ but it was too hot.

9. _It had just come out of the oven_ so it was too hot.

10. _She left the soup_ because it was too hot.

B WORD WORK

Add the missing vowel phonemes.

1. s m o o t h l y
2. c h e e r f u l
3. p e a c e f u l

> **PART B Focus**
> 1–3: vowel phonemes; familiar suffixes
> 4–5: synonyms
> 6–8: doubling letters when adding **ed** or **ing**
> 9–10: working out meaning

4. Which word means **happy**? cheerful
5. Which word means **quiet**? peaceful

Underline the word that is wrongly spelt.
Write the correct spelling.

6. They went shoping. shopping
7. Let's go swiming. swimming
8. Everyone claped. clapped

Write the meaning of the words in **bold**.

9. Sitting in the hot sun, the man **dozed off**.
   'dozed off' means fell asleep

10. The jailer had a **grisly** laugh.
    'grisly' means horrible or nasty

C SENTENCE WORK

Read this sentence. **Birds build nests.**

1. Is it from a report or a story? a report
2. Give a reason for your answer. Because it gives information.

> **PART C Focus**
> 1–2: fiction; non-fiction
> 3–7: writing full sentences from notes
> 8–10: past tense in stories

Write these notes as complete sentences.

3. ants – nests – underground Ants live in nests underground.
4. hedgehog – spines, strong front claws A hedgehog has spines and strong front claws.
5. baby goat – kid A baby goat is called a kid.
6. wool – sheep – farms Wool comes from sheep kept on farms.
7. lizard – short legs, tail A lizard has short legs and a tail.

Cross out the words that sound wrong. Write the correct words.

8. Once upon a time there ~~is~~ a little girl ~~call~~ Bella. was called
9. Long ago there ~~lives~~ an old man who ~~have~~ no money. lived had
10. There ~~is~~ once a farmer who ~~goes~~ to market every week. was went

Section 3 Test 9

A WARM-UP

Write three words that rhyme with the word in **bold**.

1	**here**	cheer	peer	dear
2	**yawn**	born	dawn	corn
3	**bird**	word	third	heard

Mrs Amin was going to the shop. What happened?

4 On the way _she met Mrs Bradley._

5 Suddenly, _it started to rain._

6 When she got to the shop, _it was_

closed.

Put these words together to make four compound words.

teller book story case shelf

7 _bookcase_

8 _bookshelf_

9 _storybook_

10 _storyteller_

PART A Focus
1–3: rhyme; correct spelling of vowel phonemes
4–6: using connectives; writing sentences that are complete, with ideas that follow on
7–10: compound words

B WORD WORK

Complete the word sum.

1 **pop + ed** = _popped_

2 **sit + ing** = _sitting_

3 **like + ing** = _liking_

4 **live + ed** = _lived_

The same letters are missing from all these rhyming words. Write them in.

5 f r i g h t

6 n i g h t

7 b r i g h t

8 l i g h t

PART B Focus
1–4: rules for adding ed and ing to verbs
5–8: using igh
9–10: choosing synonyms for effect

9 Underline the word that sounds smallest.

small   little   <u>minute</u>   tiny

10 Underline the word that sounds biggest.

large   big   <u>enormous</u>   great

C SENTENCE WORK

Finish the sentence.

1 Take a rest when _you are tired._

2 There was no-one there when _we went inside._

3 You can only build a snowman when _there is lots of snow._

4 He was scared when _the lights went out._

Write the sentence as a question.

5 We can go swimming. _Can we go swimming?_

6 I can help clean the car. _Can I help clean the car?_

7 You do know Alia. _Do you know Alia?_

PART C Focus
1–4: forming complex sentences using when
5–7: reordering words to form questions; adding question marks
8–10: commas in a list

Add three more items to the sentence. Add commas.

8 In my pocket I have a bus ticket, _a marble, two paper clips and some sweets._

9 In the winter I wear my coat, _gloves, scarf and a woolly hat._

10 You need a pencil, _a ruler, crayons and some paper._

X DEFINITIVE ANSWER   X SAMPLE ANSWER

A WARM-UP

Write the start of each sentence.

1 _I go to bed_ when I am sleepy.

2 _It was still dark_ when Sam woke up.

3 _You need an umbrella_ when it rains.

4 _There was a great view_ when we got to the top.

5 Make six words using these phonemes only.

b c h l n ow

bow	_cow_	_how_
low	_own_	_bowl_

Add the missing vowel phoneme.

Clue: five senses

6 s _e_ e

7 h _e a_ r

8 t _a_ s t e

9 s m _e_ l l

10 t _o u_ c h

> **PART A Focus**
> **1–4:** forming sentences that make sense and are correctly punctuated; using **when**
> **5:** blending phonemes; different sounds made by **ow** grapheme
> **6–10:** vowel phonemes

B WORD WORK

Change the first phoneme of the word in **bold** to make two words that rhyme with it.

1 **c h a i r** _fair_ _pair_

2 **b e a r** _pear_ _wear_

3 **s h a r e** _dare_ _glare_

Add the missing ending.

ly ful

4 He said he would glad _ly_ help.

5 The hairbrush was use _ful_ .

6 They had a love _ly_ time.

7 The old man was forget _ful_ .

Write the pairs of words that have the same meaning.

leap throw jump

shiver hurl shake

> **PART B Focus**
> **1–3:** different spellings of **air** phoneme
> **4–7:** common suffixes
> **8–10:** synonyms; less common words

8 _leap_ and _jump_

9 _throw_ and _hurl_

10 _shiver_ and _shake_

C SENTENCE WORK

Write the next sentence. It must follow on from the first.

1 **Add the sugar to the flour. Next,** _add the eggs._

2 **Jack slowly climbed the beanstalk. Eventually,** _he reached the top._

3 **We stopped for an ice cream. After that,** _we walked up the hill._

4 **Aziz sat in his armchair. Suddenly,** _there was a knock at the door._

What kind of text is the sentence from? **a story   a recount   instructions**

5 1 is from _instructions._

6 2 is from _a story._

7 3 is from _a recount._

8 4 is from _a story._

9 Add punctuation and capitals to the rhyme.

W
what is blue?

T
the sky is blue.

W
what is green?

T
the grass is green.

10 Add the capital letters to this address.

M J   D
mr james doyle

        H   S
51 hill street

F   FH JK
fordham fh5 3jk

> **PART C Focus**
> **1–4:** connectives; sentences linked by sense
> **5–8:** identifying text types
> **9:** capital letters, full stops and question marks
> **10:** using capital letters

X **DEFINITIVE ANSWER**   X **SAMPLE ANSWER**

Section 3 Test 11

A WARM-UP

Write the correct word.

play loves washes clean

1   They _____clean_____ the windows.

2   She _____loves_____ football.

3   We _____play_____ games.

4   He _____washes_____ the car.

5   Write three words you might use to describe a wizard.

_____mysterious_____   _____old_____   _____wise_____

Add the missing letter.

i o u

6   l **i** m e   8   h **u** g e

7   c **u** b e   9   h **o** l e

> **PART A Focus**
> **1–4:** grammatical agreement; making sense
> **5:** vocabulary choice
> **6–9:** vowel phonemes; modifying e
> **10:** word building; vowel phonemes

10 Tick the vowel phonemes that could go in this word.

b _ _ s t

u r ✓   e a ✓   a i   o a ✓   o r

B WORD WORK

Add the missing vowel phoneme.

ear air

1   a p p **e a** r   3   f **a i** r

2   n **e a** r   4   f **e a** r

5   Which words go with these prefixes?

dis un

dis _appear_   un _fair_

6   Which words go with these suffixes?

ful ly

fear ful   _near_ ly

> **PART B Focus**
> **1–4:** vowel phonemes
> **5–6:** prefixes and suffixes
> **7:** identifying spelling errors
> **8–10:** spelling strategies; technical words (science)

7   Cross out the words that are wrongly spelt.

The ~~bizy~~ bee ~~floo rownd~~ the ~~gardin~~.

Write the correct spellings.

busy   _flew_   _round_   _garden_

Add the second syllable.

8   i n v **e s** t i g a t e   *Clue: explore*

9   m a g **n** i f y   *Clue: make bigger*

10 e x **a m** i n e   *Clue: look closely at*

C SENTENCE WORK

Complete the sentence.

1   If you heat water in a kettle, _it will boil._

2   _Water freezes_ _____ when it is very cold.

3   Plants cannot grow in a desert because _there is no water._

4   Use water to wash your clothes when _they get dirty._

Cross out one of the words in the sentence. Write one of these words instead.

leaps rushes prowls soars flutters

5   A man ~~jumps~~ over the wall.   _leaps_

6   A bird ~~flies~~ high above.   _soars_

7   A tiger ~~walks~~ in the grass.   _prowls_

8   A butterfly ~~flaps~~ its wings.   _flutters_

9   A river ~~runs~~ down the hill.   _rushes_

> **PART C Focus**
> **1–4:** using connectives to form sentences that explain
> **5–9:** synonyms; adventurous word choice
> **10:** demarcating sentence boundaries

10 This is the beginning of a report. Check it for capital letters, full stops and question marks.

~~in~~ ^I ~~july~~ ^J it is often hot and sunny. ~~in~~ ^I ~~january~~ ^J it is cold. ~~why~~ ^W is this?

X DEFINITIVE ANSWER   X SAMPLE ANSWER

Section 3　Test 12

A　WARM-UP

Complete the sentence.

1　It was dark so ___I put on the light.___

2　I was tired so ___I went to bed.___

Add the missing letters.

e a

3　n e t b a l l

4　b e a n s t a l k

5　h e a d s t a n d

6　s e a s h e l l

> **PART A Focus**
> **1–2:** compound sentences using **so** to show resulting actions
> **3–6:** compound words; vowel phonemes
> **7–8:** rhyme; spelling patterns
> **9–10:** use of capitals

Write two words that rhyme with the words in **bold**.

7　**found**　**round**　___hound___　___ground___

8　**face**　**trace**　___pace___　___grace___

Rewrite the sentence with the capital letters in the correct places.

9　last Year i was in mrs neil's Class.
　___Last year I was in Mrs Neil's class.___

10　now i Am In mr owen's class.
　___Now I am in Mr Owen's class.___

B　WORD WORK

Add the missing letters.

ou ow

1　s h o w e r   o f   r a i n

2　c o u n t i n g   s h e e p

3　b o u n c y   c a s t l e

4　f r o w n i n g   f a c e

> **PART B Focus**
> **1–4:** different spellings of vowel phoneme **ow**
> **5–7:** high-frequency words
> **8–10:** working out the meaning of less common words

Underline the correct spelling.

5　warter　worter　<u>water</u>　worta

6　wont　<u>want</u>　whant　whont

7　werk　werc　whork　<u>work</u>

Write the meaning of the word in **bold**.

8　They were **astonished** by his idea.
　'astonished' means ___surprised or amazed___

9　"Stop!" **pleaded** the captain.
　'pleaded' means ___begged___

10　The ship had been **wrecked**.
　'wrecked' means ___destroyed or ruined___

C　SENTENCE WORK

Finish the sentence.

1　We had a long wait at the airport. Finally, ___they called our flight.___

2　The Prince walked for many days. Finally, ___he reached the castle.___

3　Leave the cake to cool. Finally, ___sprinkle it with sugar.___

Add two describing words.

4　The ___little___ girl crept into the ___quiet___ wood.

5　The ___poor___ ___old___ man fell down the steps.

6　One ___rainy___ night, the ___wicked___ man ran away.

Underline what the character says.

7　<u>"Are you telling the truth?"</u> asked Salma.

8　<u>"I don't like cabbage,"</u> moaned Sophie.

9　<u>"You must keep your promise,"</u> said the King.

10　<u>"What is your name?"</u> asked the teacher.

> **PART C Focus**
> **1–3:** using the connective **finally** to link sentences
> **4–6:** using descriptive words
> **7–10:** understanding speech marks

Remind the pupil to complete Section 3 of the Progress chart on page 46 of the workbook.

Schofield & Sims English Skills 1

Section 3 Writing task assessment sheet: How to keep healthy

Name		Class/Set
Teacher's name		Date

Sentence structure and punctuation

	Always/often	Sometimes	Never
Writes in clear and separate sentences			
Uses simple and compound sentences			
Uses connectives to extend sentences: e.g., **but**, **so**, **because** (to give a reason); **when** (to make a time link)			
Full stops mark end of simple and compound sentences			
Capital letters mark start of sentences			
Capital letters used for names, titles, etc.			
Uses commas in a list			
Maintains present tense in report			
Sentences grammatically accurate (e.g., agreement)			

Composition and effect

Sounds like non-fiction writing (e.g., conveying information)			
Includes a range of relevant information			
Ideas are organised			
Ideas are expanded (e.g., over two or three linked sentences)			
Uses relevant technical vocabulary			

Spelling

Plausible spelling of phonically regular words			
Correct spelling of vowel phonemes			
Compound words or words with phonically regular syllables are correct			
High-frequency words are correct			
Spelling of words with prefixes (**un**, **dis**) or suffixes (**ful**, **ly**) is correct			
Verb endings **ing** and **ed** are correct (e.g., double letters, dropping final **e**)			
Spelling of plurals is correct (e.g., **s** or **es**)			

Writing task summary

Schofield & Sims English Skills 1

Section 3 Completed proofreading task: Wendy the witch

Name	Class/Set
Teacher's name	Date

There was ~~wonce~~ [e] a little witch calld [e] ~~wendy~~ [W]. she [S] livd [e] in a tiny howse [u]. in the wuds [oo].

She had green hair. And [a] a green face. She know [e] lots of spels [l]. But [b] thay [e] was [ere]

gud [oo] spells. Not [n] bad ~~wones~~.

Every day she put on her hat, cloke [a] and ~~poyntid~~ [pointed] shoos [e]. and went of [f] into the wuds [oo].

wendy [W] ~~is~~ [was] happy and chearfull [e] so evryone [e] liket [d] her. the [T] anmals [i] was [ere] not scaird [e] off her.

she [S] always stoped [P] to talk to them.

Proofreading task summary

Section 3 tasks summary

Full list of the Schofield & Sims English Skills books

Workbooks

For Key Stage 2:

English Skills 1	978 07217 1175 1
English Skills 2	978 07217 1176 8
English Skills 3	978 07217 1177 5
English Skills 4	978 07217 1178 2
English Skills 5	978 07217 1179 9
English Skills 6	978 07217 1180 5

The same workbooks, with covers designed for older users – at Key Stage 3 and beyond:

Essential English Skills 1	978 07217 1188 1
Essential English Skills 2	978 07217 1189 8
Essential English Skills 3	978 07217 1190 4
Essential English Skills 4	978 07217 1191 1
Essential English Skills 5	978 07217 1192 8
Essential English Skills 6	978 07217 1193 5

Answers

Suitable for use with both **English Skills** and **Essential English Skills**:

English Skills 1 Answers	978 07217 1181 2
English Skills 2 Answers	978 07217 1182 9
English Skills 3 Answers	978 07217 1183 6
English Skills 4 Answers	978 07217 1184 3
English Skills 5 Answers	978 07217 1185 0
English Skills 6 Answers	978 07217 1186 7

Teacher's Guide

The **Teacher's Guide** contains the **Workbook descriptors**, **Entry test** and many other useful items suitable for use with both **English Skills** and **Essential English Skills**:

| English Skills Teacher's Guide | 978 07217 1187 4 |

Also available

Mental Arithmetic (for Key Stage 2) and **Essential Mental Arithmetic** (for Key Stage 3 and beyond) are similar in format to **English Skills** and **Essential English Skills**, providing intensive maths practice.

 For further information about both series, and for details of the **I can do** teaching method, which can be used with all the books mentioned on this page, visit **www.schofieldandsims.co.uk**